AUTHORS AND TITLES

That the concept of authorship is a difficult and
confused one in cataloguing theory is of the utmost
importance and is, in general, completely overlooked.
In the whole discussions of the conference *(ICCP)*
no one really raised the question of what is meant
by authorship. It is one of the unformulated
assumptions of most discussions of cataloguing that
we all know what is meant by authorship. It is true
that the concept of personal authorship is
reasonably clear as applied to a book by a single
author, but it becomes more and more tenuous
as it is pursued through joint authorship, multiple
authorship, corporate authorship,
and, finally, if it does not vanish
completely as a reliable guide, it is so meta-
morphosed as to be hardly recognisable.

Leonard Jolley

Thoughts after Paris, 1963

AUTHORS AND TITLES

An analytical study of the author concept
in codes of cataloguing rules in the
English language, from that of the British
Museum in 1841 to the Anglo-American
Cataloguing rules 1967.

JAMES A TAIT MA MSc FLA
UNIVERSITY OF STRATHCLYDE

ARCHON BOOKS & CLIVE BINGLEY

FIRST PUBLISHED 1969 BY CLIVE BINGLEY LTD
THIS EDITION SIMULTANEOUSLY PUBLISHED IN THE USA
BY ARCHON BOOKS THE SHOE STRING PRESS INC
995 SHERMAN AVENUE HAMDEN CONNECTICUT 06514
PRINTED IN THE UK
COPYRIGHT © JAMES A TAIT 1969
208 00876 4

CONTENTS

Page

ABBREVIATIONS (used for codes of cataloguing rules)

AA (1908)   Library Association. Cataloguing rules:
                   author and title entries; English ed.
                   London, 1908.

ALA (1941)   American Library Association. ALA catalog
                   rules: author and title entries; prelim.
                   2nd ed. Chicago, 1941.

ALA (1949)   American Library Association. ALA
                   cataloging rules for author and title
                   entries; 2nd ed. Chicago, 1949.

CCR (1960)   American Library Association. Code of
                   cataloging rules, author and title entry:
                   an unfinished draft. Chicago, 1960.

ICCP (1961)   International Federation of Library Assoc-
                   iations. International conference on
                   cataloguing principles, Paris, 9th-18th
                   October 1961. Report. London, 1963.
                   Reprinted 1969.

AACR (1967)   American Library Association. Anglo-
                   American cataloguing rules, prepared by the
                   American Library Association, the
                   Library of Congress, the Library
                   Association, and the Canadian Library
                   Association: British text. London, 1967.

1
FUNCTIONS OF THE AUTHOR CATALOGUE

The author catalogue is generally considered essential in any library. In some of the older institutions it is the only form of catalogue supplied. For example, the British Museum provides no subject guidance to the printed books in its stock before 1881; only an author catalogue is provided, with entries for titles in the absence of authors. The history of cataloguing has seen many author codes, but there have been few subject codes, much more thought and research having been devoted to the problem of author entry than to subject entry. By and large, author catalogues are considered essential, though the reasons why this should be so are somewhat obscure and often confused. It is the purpose of this work to examine the principles of authorship for the construction of author catalogues of libraries, and to trace the history of these principles in the main author cataloguing codes in the English language from 1841 until the present.

Two reasons seem to suggest themselves as primarily responsible for the importance attaching to author catalogues. First, the name of the author as printed on the spine and the title-page of a book is the most easily identifiable feature of a book. 'It is generally accepted that the author catalogue, or some variation of it . . . is supreme in value and importance, because it is the only catalogue from which a reader can be perfectly certain of ascertaining whether a library has a particular book, assuming that he has the author's name correctly, for the author's name is the one indisputable thing about a book . . .'.[1] Hence the reason for the author catalogue, as an inventory of the bookstock of a library in which each item is listed under its most identifiable feature. This is equivalent to

1   Henry A Sharp, Cataloguing; 3rd ed rev, London, 1944, p 19.

the storekeeper maintaining an inventory of his stock by name of thing or product stocked. The inventory function of the author catalogue was its sole function in early medieval times when books were precious manuscripts and had to be accounted for. The concept of the author catalogue as providing a guide to the contents of a library is a much more recent development. The second reason for the importance attached to author catalogues is the assumption that the catalogue-user will 'group' books by author rather than by title, *ie* he will be more interested in works sharing a common author than he will be in works sharing a common title, or common first word in their titles. This is an assumption made by cataloguers in the past, the editors of AACR (1967) accepted this as well. In recent years there has, however, been a questioning of this inherited assumption — a questioning in favour of title entry, which we will allude to later.

The other identifiable feature of a literary work is its title, again appearing on the title-page, usually also in a shortened form on the half-title page as well, and also on the spine of the book. As a primary identifying characteristic of a book, the title has certain drawbacks. It is liable to change through translation, transliteration, revision, etc. Being longer, the title is not usually so accurately remembered as the name of the author of a book. Also, with the Anglo-American tradition of entry of titles under their first words other than articles, accuracy of memory is put at a premium. There may be one or more words coming later in the title which are much more memorable, but unless the first (non-article) word of a title is remembered, such a work cannot be found in the catalogue. One alternative to this 'mechanical arrangement', as it is called bythe Germans, is entry under the most significant word in the title, which itself may be open to different interpretations. The British Museum adopts significant word entry for titles, and has a complicated series of eliminating rules for the choice of entry word for titles. The Germans themselves adopt a different solution and enter titles according to their grammatical structure, *ie* under the first noun in the title not standing in an attributive or adverbial relationship.

Neither the sole nor the primary function of an author catalogue is, however, to list books and other documents under ·

their most identifiable features. The definition of authorship usually accepted infers a wider and more important function for the author catalogue. Any literary production is the printed expression of one or more than one person's thought and research, and it is usually considered to be an important function of the author catalogue to recognise and record this fact. This we shall call the 'intellectual responsibility' concept of author cataloguing. To deny this would amount to limiting the function of an author catalogue merely to that of an inventory. The fact that a work is the embodiment of a person's thought is of supreme importance in relation to that work. The subject content gains added interest as the product of the intellection of one or more named persons. In the case of imaginative literature this is particularly true.

Too rigid adherence to either principle can result in a distortion of the catalogue. If the principle of intellectual responsibility is adhered to too strictly to the extent of attempting at all costs to enter a work under the name of an author, we get the result seen in CCR (1960) where examples are given of entry under the 'performer' as the author of the compositions on a phonodisc, and the actor as the author of a book containing photographs of himself in his various roles.[1] This would seem to suggest that for certain types of material author entry may not be suitable, and that the attempt to find an author entry at all costs can lead to some illogical conclusions in a catalogue that claims to be constructed on purely logical principles. On the other hand, if we merely base our author catalogues on what we regard as the most identifiable feature of a work being catalogued, we may find ourselves producing a hybrid catalogue, neither completely author, title, nor anything else. There may be cases, especially in multiple authorship, where it is almost impossible and certainly undesirable to ascribe authorship. In such cases, some substitute for authorship must be found, but to base all one's catalogue on the most identifiable feature of a literary work is to produce a catalogue similar to some medieval catalogues which entered works indiscriminately under author, title, or even subject. Even in a catalogue constructed logically from the principle of intellectual responsibility, it is necessary to draw up a list of priorities in relation to the alternative

1 Johannes L Dewton. The grand illusion. *Library Journal* May 1 1961, p 1723.

features of a work which may be chosen for entry other than the name of the author.

These two criteria for the author catalogue — identification tag, and intellectual responsibility, have in the past caused considerable confusion as to the primary functions of an author catalogue. With many books and documents there is no difficulty, the work being by one author named on the title-page, and called by one unchanging title. In these circumstances the two principles are not in conflict, but in other cases where the above criteria do not hold, we may have to pursue one principle at the expense of the other. Can we accept the principle of intellectual responsibility and still subscribe to the finding-list function of the catalogue, or must we pursue one at the expense of the other? The history of cataloguing codes for author entry over the last one hundred and fifty years has revealed conflicting and changing views as to the merits of the two principles of author cataloguing.

Definition and scope of author, editor, compiler, etc
The definition of 'author' which one accepts will, of course, be determined by one's concept of the primary function of the author catalogue. If the function of the author catalogue is taken to be that of ascribing works to those primarily responsible for their creation, then authorship must be defined in terms of the person or persons, or corporate body primarily responsible for a work's existence. Generally, in those codes which base their rules on intellectual responsibility for a work this is so. For example, AA (1908) defines authorship in the following terms:

> The writer of a book, as distinct from translator, editor, etc. . . Corporate bodies may be considered the authors of publications issued in their name or by their authority.

ALA (1949) adheres generally to the same definition, but widens the scope to include artistic and musical productions as well as literary. Cutter's definition is also similar, as is that of ICCP (1961). The definition of AACR (1967) is similar:

> By author is meant the person or corporate body chiefly responsible for the creation of the intellectual or artistic content of a work.

10

It is of some significance that neither the British Museum code nor CCR (1960) attempts to define authorship, because these are the two codes which lay most emphasis on the information given on the title-page of the book being catalogued. CCR (1960) in particular attempts to compromise between the intellectual responsibility concept and the information as given on the title-page of a book, largely because, in previous codes, too strict an adherence to the intellectual responsibility concept resulted in entries under headings which would be very difficult to locate in a catalogue if the only information one had was that to be found on the title-page of the book being catalogued. This point will be discussed at greater length later.

All the codes which define authorship in terms of primary intellectual responsibility for a work extend the definition include editors and compilers of works by a number of different authors. Editorship covers a wide area of responsibility, ranging from preparation for the press to the responsibility for the shape and form which a particular work takes. In some instances, the role of editor is very similar to that of compiler − a much more limited term. A compiler would appear to be responsible for bringing together in book form the work of a number of persons, or for a selection from one person's writing, without amending or retouching the original text in any way, whereas editorship would seem to imply some reworking of the original text(s). Where the original work is by one author, by the principle of intellectual responsibility, the editor cannot be held responsible for the result of the intellection of another person, though he may have commented upon it, selected from it, or edited it textually. In this situation the problem of primary responsibility is clearly defined, and it serves as an adequate principle for the cataloguing of such publications. All codes are agreed on ths point. There are some rather marginal cases, however. For example, in certain publications which reproduce the work of an artist, architect, photographer, etc, the work of the editor may be more important than that of the original author.

When we come to multiple authorship, the problems and their solutions are by no means as clear-cut. On the face of it, it would be difficult to maintain that the person who collects together the writings of several authors can be held in any way responsible for their intellection. The original authors are responsible,

11

and in such circumstances, the title would appear to be the correct heading. An example would be the various Oxford books of verse. Most of the codes, however, ignore this reasonably straightforward solution, with the exception of ICCP (1961) where a majority of the delegates voted for title entry in such circumstances.[1]. The other codes prefer entry under an editor or compiler, by stating that an editor or compiler who collects the writings of several persons is responsible for the presentation of the results. This is the essence of the wider definition of authorship in AA (1908) and ALA (1949) *ie* responsibility for the shape and form that the work takes.

By extending the definition of authorship in this manner two entirely different interpretations of the term 'author' would seem to be operating: 1 intellectual responsibility for a piece of work; 2 responsibility for collecting the works of others into book form. One is not, however, intellectually responsible for the writings which one collects into book form, as one would be for an original piece of work. In such circumstances the editor or compiler is chosen because he is the unifying factor which gives the particular work its existence. To argue that he is intellectually responsible for the thought content of the volume which he edits or compiles hardly bears examination. Entry under editor is also entry under the most prominent identification tag on the title-page. The name of an editor or compiler is often the only personal name on the title-page of a collection. This view of entry under compiler or editor for the main entry for a collection is re-inforced when one examines the codes of rules. AA (1908) and ALA (1949) would only enter a collection under the name of an editor if his name appears in the publication itself. CCR (1960) and AACR (1967) are even more precise and exact, demanding the appearance of the name of an editor on the title-page before entry can be made under him.

In many circumstances, entry under the title would give a much more sought-after heading, and would avoid confusion of the functions of authorship with those of editorship. Such a form of entry would also bring the rule into line with the rule for periodicals and other serial publications, which are almost invariably entered under their titles.

1   See Statement of Principles, no 10.3.

12

Distinction between work and book

Lubetzky in CCR (1960) first makes clear the distinction between *work* and *book,* in as much as he discerns that the object to be catalogued may appear in various physical forms – a book, a record, a tape, or in microform. It is the distinction between the intellectual product and its physical manifestation. It is fairly obvious that cataloguers and publishers alike are interested in the intellectual product, rather than in a given quantity of paper, celluloid film or reel of plastic.

Having established this point, a proviso must immediately be added to the effect that this only holds good on the assumption that we are dealing with physical bibliographical units. The work in the shape of one of Bernard Shaw's plays *The devil's disciple* is published as a separate bibliographical unit, but it does also exist as part of the volume of Shaw's plays entitled *Three plays for puritans.* This may be the only edition of the work in a small library, but assuming that no analytical entries are to be made, we are back to the book rather than the work. It could be argued that a collection or anthology has an independent existence quite apart from that of its parts, though in the previous section we argued against this point of view.[1, 2]

The distinction between the work and the book also lies at the root of the distinction between cataloguing by the intellectual responsibility concept and cataloguing by the title-page tag. The inventory concept of cataloguing assumes interest in the book, the individual volume, rather than the work or the intellection of which the book is the expression. That the work is of more permanent interest and importance than its embodiment in any particular book would hardly seem worthy of argument, yet confusion between the two concepts has given rise to inconsistencies within many of the codes of rules for author cataloguing, as will be discussed later. The distinction is also unfortunately evident in the forms of entry found in library catalogues and those in many booktrade bibliographies and catalogues. The booktrade is interested primarily in the book, the individual volume, and is not so concerned as cataloguers

1 Theodore C Hines. Comment on draft code. *Library resources* 5 (3) Summer 1961, 237-240.
2 L Jolley, International conference on cataloguing principles II. Thoughts after Paris. *Journal of documentation* 19 (2) June 1963, 52.

are in ascribing intellectual responsibility to a particular person for a given work. The difference is unfortunate, since many catalogue users gain their first information about a work from a booktrade catalogue or bibliography. Their subsequent tracing of many such works in a library catalogue may be hampered if the catalogue has been constructed on the basis of the intellectual responsibility concept, and some technically correct heading used for a particular work. For the librarian, too, the many divergences between the two types of cataloguing may lead to difficulties in checking publishers' catalogues, and even result in double ordering. The divergences are usually less when the national bibliography is compiled within or under the auspices of the national library, for example, the British National Bibliography.[1]

The distinction between a work and a book is also inherent in the differentiation between the 'literary unit' and the 'bibliographic unit'.[2] By the literary unit is meant the assemblage under one heading in the catalogue of all the entries for works by the one author, no matter how he chooses to name himself on the title-pages of his works. The literary unit is recognised by AA (1908), ALA (1949), and the Prussian Instructions, but is ignored by the British Museum.[3] On the other hand, the 'bibliographic unit' refers to the collection of all entries for the various versions of the same work under one uniform heading, both under authors' names, and in the main sequence of the catalogue. The latter concept is ignored for the most part by AA (1908) and ALA (1949), but recognised as relevant by the British Museum. Most cataloguers would accept the necessity of the bibliographic unit, while expressing some doubt about the validity of the literary unit, if this means entering authors under forms of name under which it is doubtful if the majority of catalogue users would look. At first glance

1 Andrew D Osborn. Relation between cataloguing principles and principles applicable to other forms of bibliographic work. ICCP report (1963), working paper no 1.
2 Seymour Lubetzky. Cataloging rules and principles, Washington, 1953.
3 Julia Pettee.The development of authorship entry and the formulation of authorship rules as found in the Anglo-American code. *Library quarterly,* (3) July 1936, 285.

it might appear as if acceptance of the literary unit follows from the initial acceptance of the concept of intellectual responsibility. But the basis of cataloguing under author does not also imply that any given author should be entered under one uniform heading. All codes are agreed that the application of the literary unit will apply to differences in the forms of an author's name, for example, the use and non-use of a hyphen between middle name and surname, noblemen always entered under family name or title, never both. Where the codes disagree is in the extension of the principle to authors who use more than one name, for example, a real name and one or more pseudonym. The difference is really only one of degree. One real difference of opinion is over what should be chosen for the literary unit. AA (1908) and ALA (1949) prefer the full, real, baptismal name of an author, while later codes tend to prefer the name by which an author is identified most commonly on the title-pages of his works or in reference sources.

The bibliographic unit is generally accepted cataloguing practice because of acceptance of the work as the unit in cataloguing rather than the book. This principle is frequently ignored in AA (1908) and ALA (1949). It becomes particularly important in the case of title entry for anonymous works. Both AA (1908) and ALA (1949) have a long series of rules covering the entry of anonymous works, for example, where the first word of the title may be spelled in more than one way; translations of anonymous works; anonymous classics; works known by a standardised form of title, for example the *Bible.* The fact that AA (1908) and ALA (1949) make these elaborate provisions merely emphasises the importance of the concept, and is a surprising element in these two codes in view of the fact that they ignore its presence in all rules for works by named authors.

The use of form headings in the author catalogue also has some bearing on the concept of the 'bibliographic unit'. Such usage is only legitimate as a last resource in the construction of the bibliographic unit, when both the author element and the title element, particularly the latter, are insufficient. But even the latter situation can be entered for by the use of uniform titles as in AACR (1967). What is less legitimate is the use of
15

form headings or form subheadings to construct 'extra-biblio-graphical units', *ie* the grouping together of entries for publications which for one reason or another, the cataloguer wishes to bring together in the catalogue, but which, biblio-graphically, do not form a unit, for example, the many form headings in the British Museum rules — Directories, Diction-aries, Ephemerides, etc.

Historical background

The history of the development of library catalogues exhibits a gradual and sometimes hesitant development from the inventorial function through the finding list function to the final development of the intellectual responsibility concept in the late nineteenth century.[1] Throughout the middle ages and for some time after, the sole function of the catalogue was considered to be inventorial. A manuscript was a precious possession to a cathedral or monastery; it was costly, and in themonastic institutions, where in the middle ages most of the manuscripts were made and held, a careful list or inventory was considered a necessity. Usually the manuscripts were listed in the order in which they were received into the mona-stery in the form of 'donation books'. The inventory function of such lists was reinforced by the bare details given for each item listed, and with the authors' christian names preceding the surnames. The fact that miscellaneous volumes of separate manuscripts were bound together, as was often the rule, and were catalogued merely under the first work in the collection or volume gives added weight to the inventory function of the early monastic catalogues.'Catalogs were made by librarians largely for their own use and had one simple function, that of an inventory or a collection of lists showing the holdings. The form and arrangement of the entries were arbitrary'.[2]

The sixteenth century witnessed great political, social and economic upheavals, but library catalogues still followed their medieval precursors and were obviously incapable of supporting the new scholarship of Galileo, Descartes, Bacon, Kepler, etc.

1   Ruth E Strout. The development of the catalogue and cataloging codes. *Library quarterly* 26 (4) October 1956, 254-275
2   Seymour Lubetzky. The development of cataloging rules. *Library trends* 2 (2) October 1953, 179-186.

It was unfortunately not librarians, but the new scholars themselves who initiated new ideas in cataloguing practice to produce
some kind of index to the world's learning. In the sixteenth
century we see the start of the idea of the catalogue as a finding
list or index to literature in the work of Conrad Gesner,
botanist and bibliographer.[1] Gesner laid considerable stress
on the value of author indexes to classified subject lists. He
inverted the names of the authors in his indexes to bring the
surname to the front. Florian Trefler, a Benedictine monk of
Augsburg, was critical of the difficulties he experienced in
libraries of finding information about their bookstocks when
they were not catalogued. He devised a classification scheme
for the books and for the catalogue of them, an essential part
of the catalogue being an alphabetical author index.[2] Andrew
Maunsell, the English bookseller, in 1595 insisted that one should
be able to find books in the catalogue under their authors'
names, translators, and subjects.[3] Maunsell's work represented
the first germs of a code of cataloguing rules for authors.

At the beginning of the seventeenth century Sir Thomas
Bodley was directing the compilation of the catalogues of the
then new Bodleian Library, emphasising the point of view of
the user, and insisting upon author rather than subject catalogues.
Gradually throughout the seventeenth century catalogues were
beginning to be looked upon as finding-lists rather than as mere
inventories. Authors were entered regularly under their surnames,
and often arranged chronologically. For example, in his preface
to the 1674 Catalogue of the Bodleian Library, one of its most
eminent librarians, Thomas Hyde, urges the entry of authors
under their surnames even if this will cause inconvenience to the
user where an author is known by his forename only.[4]

The concept of the catalogue as a finding-list has persisted
until the present day, and is indeed one of its most important

1   Conrad Gesner. Bibliography of Latin, Greek and Hebrew authors, 1545, *and*
Pandectarium, sive partitionum universalium, libri XXI, 1548.
2   Florian Trefler. Methodus exhibens per varios indices et classes subinde . . .
brevem, facilem, imitabilem, ordinationem, 1560.
3   Andrew Maunsell. First and second parts of a catalogue of English printed
books, 1595.
4   Julia Pettee. *op cit,* pp 220-290

functions. Its further development into something more than a finding-list did not occur until the middle of the nineteenth century in the hands of Panizzi of the British Museum, followed by Jewett of the Smithsonian Institution in Washington, and above all by Cutter of the Boston Athenaeum. The functions of the catalogue as viewed by Cutter at the end of the nineteenth century are summarised as follows:

a To provide an indication if the library has a given book by a named author.

b To indicate what books a library has by a named author.'

Almost identical objectives were repeated by ICCP eighty years later in 1961.[2] Function *a* underlines the finding-list function of the catalogue, while function *b* takes cognisance of the concept of intellectual responsibility. In the great majority of books the two functions coincide, and it is only in the few cases that conflict between the two objectives occurs, *ie* when the information as given on the title-page does not prominently and clearly indicate the person or body primarily responsible for the intellectual content of a work, *eg* in the case of multiple authorship, with no clear indication of the principal author, corporate authorship with both the name of a corporate body and a person named on the title-page, etc. In such cases, the basing of the catalogue heading on the intellectual responsibility concept may well impair its function as a direct finding-list. This difficulty was, of course, appreciated by the giants of nineteenth century cataloguing, mentioned above, and they made provision for it by developing the concept of added entries, which, by the end of the century, had become standard cataloguing practice, and whose function had been assigned to indexes by Florian Trefler and most of the other pioneers of the sixteenth and seventeenth centuries already mentioned. By the end of the nineteenth century, in the United States, the card catalogue was gaining in popularity over the printed book catalogue, and became supreme after the introduction of the Library of Congress printed card distribution scheme in 1901. The economic operation of any centrally distributed printed card scheme depends on one form for all types of entry. The

1 Charles Ammi Cutter. Rules for a dictionary catalogue; 4th ed, rewritten, 1904.
2 International Conference on Cataloguing Principles, Paris, 9th — 18th October 1961, 1963, p 25.

form used by the Library of Congress for the standard entry was the main author entry, *ie* with a heading for the name of the author followed in separate paragraphs by the title and other details of the work being catalogued. Added entries were made merely by using another copy of the main entry and adding the appropriate heading at the top. The added entry cards were thus replicas of the main entry card with the addition of the added entry heading. Thus, the main entry heading intruded between the added entry heading and the title. This practice of unit entry more or less abolished the distinction between main and added entries in the multiple entry catalogues for which the cards were designed. The Library of Congress followed Cutter in using the main entry to ascribe intellectual responsibility for the work being catalogued, and the finding list function of the catalogue was to be performed by the added entries, which before unit cataloguing were generally in abbreviated form. This distinction between main and added entries was adhered to in AA (1908) and also in ALA (1949) when for all practical purposes the need for such a distinction had more or less disappeared.

While the use of the main entry to ascribe intellectual responsibility for a publication and added entries for all other approaches may be reasonable within the main sequence of the catalogue, the method can give difficulties so far as added entries are concerned. This largely arises from the repetition of the main entry heading after the added entry heading. Therefore the sequence under a subject heading in a dictionary catalogue will automatically be according to the main entry heading, *ie* by names of authors. If the main entry heading has been constructed by some technicality based on the intellectual responsibility principle, the entry for a work may virtually be unrecognisable under the subject heading. In the main sequence of the catalogue a reference or an added entry would take care of the situation, but it would be entirely uneconomic to give a work more than one entry under a subject heading. The necessity for this would appear to have been overlooked in all the cataloguing codes.

AA (1908) and ALA (1949) even more supremely represented the high-water mark of the intellectual school of author cataloguing. After 1949 came the inevitable reaction. The attempt

19

to ascribe correctly the intellectual responsibility for a work may be a time-consuming process, especially if this is based on extra-bibliographical considerations not evident from the title-page. The attempt to track down all undiscovered pseudonyms to their real names is also time-consuming. For this and for other reasons there was a reaction against the legalistic principles upon which ALA (1949) had been constructed. It was fore-shadowed by Andrew D Osborn in his *Crisis in cataloging* of 1941.[1] The criticism of the legalistic approach was given substance by Seymour Lubetzky in his *Cataloging rules and principles* of 1953. While Lubetzky was still in favour of an author catalogue constructed on logical principles, he challenged the logic of the 1949 code. The Library of Congress had already abandoned some of the legalistic approach with its simplified cataloging procedures and 'no conflict' principle. Lubetzky continued his work with CCR (1960), though not without challenge from the larger research libraries in the United States faced with the possible relocation of many thousands of entries in their catalogue consequent onchanges of rules. AACR (1967) is, as a result, a compromise and most compromises are satisfactory to neither party.

1 Andrew D Osborn. The Crisis in cataloguing. *Library quarterly* II(4) October 1941, 393-411.

2
THE BRITISH MUSEUM RULES

The British Museum code of 1841 is undoubtedly the source of
all subsequent theories of author cataloguing. It was not called
a 'code', but entitled very simply *Rules for the compiling of the
catalogue*. The rules were drawn up by Sir Anthony Panizzi
with the assistance of eminent librarians of the day. Panizzi
was then Keeper of Printed Books, and the year 1841 saw the
publication of the first abortive volume of what was to become
of the great *General catalogue of printed books* by the end of
the century. The rules were printed in the first volume of the
catalogue. There were originally 91 rules provided primarily
for the guidance of those making entries for the new general
catalogue. By 1936, the rules had been reduced in number to
41 and the title expanded to *Rules for compiling the catalogue
of printed books, maps and music in the British Museum*. In
establishing his 91 rules, Panizzi had to overcome considerable
opposition, mainly from those who would catalogue each work
independently, and only use information found on the title-
page[1] The arguments can be read in summary form in H B
Wheatley's *How to catalogue a library*. Panizzi poured scorn on
his antagonists, pointing out the glaring inconsistencies which
would result from the practices they advocated. Yet this
opposition is partly responsible for the continued practice of
the British Museum of choosing for the heading for the main
entry only information supplied *in print* in a perfect copy of
the book being catalogued, and on that only. Rule II states:

> Titles [are] to be arranged alphabetically according to
> the English alphabet only . . . under the surname of the

1   Report of the Commissioners appointed to inquire into the constitution and
and government of the British Museum. London, 1850.

author, whenever it appears printed in the title, or
in any other part of the book.

Even works doubtfully or falsely attributed to an author on their title-pages are to be entered under the name of the supposed author, and the real name, when known, given in brackets in the description (rule XLIII). Not only must an author's name be printed in the book being catalogued before the author can be recognised by the cataloguer, but, conversely, a doubtful or fictitious author, if named in the work, would receive entry. This practice is very far removed from that of the intellectual responsibility concept, and would appear to savour more of title-page tag cataloguing. It does have its echoes, however, in later codes, particularly CCR(1960) and AACR (1967) and is a useful antidote to the excesses of the intellectual responsibility concept. However, by rule LI the work of a translator is to be entered under the name of the original author. Rule L qualifies the statement by making the proviso that the name of the original author must appear on the title-page of the translation, otherwise the work should be treated as anonymous.

Yet, in spite of what has been stated above, the 91 rules drawn up by Panizzi in 1841 did much to fix and develop the concept of authorship, although nowhere in the rules is there any definition of authorship, nor has the *General catalogue of printed books* ever been called an author catalogue. The British Museum rules have never accepted the concept of the literary unit. The name as given on the title-page will generally be accepted, even if it is a pseudonym. Rule XLI states:

> In the case of pseudonymous publications, the book
> to be catalogued under the author's feigned name; and
> his real name, if discovered, to be inserted in brackets,
> immediately after the feigned name, preceded by the
> letters *ie*

Later editions of the museum rules attempt to define and delimit the concept of a pseudonym, *cf* rule 20 in the 1936 edition.

Panizzi was, however, prepared to accept the validity of the bibliographic unit. For example, rule LII states that 'Translations are to be entered immediately after the original.'

Panizzi accepted the principle of multiple authorship, but does not appear to accept a distinction between joint and collective authorship, as AA (1908) and ALA (1949) did. Joint authorship would appear to be covered by rule III:

If more than one name occur in the title, by
which it may appear that the work is the
production of more than one person, the first
to be taken as the leading name.

By 1936, this rule had been expanded and amended in rule 15 to read as follows:

Books written in conjunction by two authors
without specification of the parts written by each,
and books in which each author, in addition to
writing a specified part, states or implies that he
has had a share in the other's contribution, are
entered under the names of both authors
conjointly, in the order in which they appear
in the book.

Where more than two authors have thus collaborated, the name of the first is taken as the heading.

Collective authorship is dealt with in Panizzi's rules by rules XLIV/XLVI:

Works of several writers, collectively published,
to be entered according to the following rules . . .
In any series of printed works, which embraces the
printed productions of various writers upon particular subjects . . . the work to be entered under the
name of the editor . . . If the editor's name do not
appear, the whole collection to be entered under
the collective title, in the same manner as anonymous works.

The museum rules thus widen the scope of author to include editor. This we have already discussed, but the points may be made that, *a* the British Museum rules do not attempt to define authorship, and *b* the use of an editor's name as author is conditional upon its appearance on the title-page. This last condition does not hold in AA (1908).

In later editions of the British Museum rules, an exception to the rule for collections is made in the case of collections of essays, etc published in honour of an individual. These are to be entered under the name of the individual concerned. The exception does not extend to memorial volumes or centenary publications. These would receive entry under editor, as for

23

other collections. The exceptions, could, however, give rise to certain anomolous situations. In the first place, to catalogue a work properly by this rule one must know whether the person in whose honour the collection has been written is deceased or still alive, though this would generally be evident from the wording of the title-page. An even more piquant situation may develop if the person in whose honour the essays have been written should happen to die while the volume is in preparation. Such a situation arose with the Sayers Memorial volume published by the Library Association in 1961[1] It was originally designed for presentation to W C Berwick Sayers, but as he died before publication, it became a memorial volume. If Sayers had lived the British Museum would have catalogued the work under Sayers, but as it was converted into a memorial volume it is catalogued under the names of its editors, Foskett and Palmer. Here we have the heading varying according to whether a person is alive or deceased. This is cataloguing by non-title-page information, and is untypical of the general practice of the British Museum.

Consistent with its non-acceptance of the literary unit as a valid cataloguing principle is the British Museum's treatment of anonymous works. The rules for anonymous works (rules XXXIII to XL) are also consistent with the general principles of rule II that only information found in the book itself being catalogued is to be used for the determination of the heading. No attempt should be made to enter an anonymous work, *ie* one in which the name of the author does not appear in the work itself, under the name of the author. This is consistent with rule II. Instead, an elaborate set of rules is given to guide the cataloguer's choice of the most significant word in the title. Rule XXXIV states that 'when no such name of a person appears, then that of any assembly, corporate body, society' board, party, sect or denomination appearing on the title to be preferred, . . . and if no such name appear, then that of any country, province, city, town or place so appearing, to be adopted as the heading.' The following rule (rule XXXV) states that 'if no name of any assembly or country . . . appear on the title, the name of the editor (if there be any) to be used as a heading; or if no editor's name appear, that of the

1   D J Foskett, and B I Palmer, eds. The Sayers memorial volume. London, 1961.

24

translator, if there be one.' Reporters are to be considered as
editors. The search here is obviously for a distinctive name
appearing on the title-page, even to the extent of accepting
the name of a translator or editor. This practice obviously is
at variance with the intellectual responsibility concept of
authorship. These rules are developed somewhat in the 1936
edition of the British Museum rules, but remain substantially
the same, with one exception. The exception appears at
the end of rule 18 in the 1936 edition of the rules and is to
the effect that anonymous editions of the classics are to be .
entered under their authors' names as a matter of common
knowledge. However, such classics have a narrow definition,
since *Erewhon,* by the example in the 1936 code, is not
treated as an exception.

The British Museum's treatment of pseudonymous works
offers an interesting commentary on the intellectual responsibility
principle. Rules XLI and XLII state in effect that where an
author uses in place of his name an official designation sufficiently clear to render his identity unmistakable entry is under
his name, otherwise entry is under the feigned name used by
the author, if it takes the form of a real name or of a single
word. In all other cases the substitute for a real name is to be
regarded as circumlocution, and the work treated as anonymous.
If an author uses one pseudonym consistently, then the literary
unit is still maintained, but if an author uses both a pseudonym
and his real name or two or more pseudonyms, the literary unit
is obviously abandoned. So far as the intellectual responsibility
problem is concerned, this is unaffected by the name or form of
name used by an author, but is affected if the work is treated
as an anonymous publication because the substitute for the
real name of an author does not satisfy the conditions laid down
by the British Museum.

Corporate authorship
On the question of corporate authorship the 91 rules of 1841
are rather equivocal. One recent interpretation of the rules is
that Panizzi contemplated a special treatment for official
documents and publications of instutions in an attempt to
regroup these publications which were still regarded as

25

anonymous under geographic or form headings [1].

On the other hand, an entirely different view of Panizzi's treatment of corporate authorship is taken by Miss Julia Pettee[2]. 'Rule IX is the most important ruling laying the foundation of our corporate entries.' The rule referred to by Miss Pettee runs as follows'-

> Any act, resolution, or other document purporting
> to be agreed upon, authorized or issued by assemblies,
> boards or corporate bodies (with the exception of
> academies, universities, learned societies and
> religious orders. . .) to be entered in distinct
> alphabetical series, under the name of the country
> or place from which they derive their denomination,
> or for want of such denomination, under the name of
> the place from whence their acts are issued.

Similarly rule XLVII states the case for entry of government publications under the name of the country:

> General collections of laws, edicts, ordinances,
> or other public acts of a similar description, to
> be entered under the name of the state or
> nation in which or by whom they were sanctioned,
> signed or promulgated. Collections extending
> only to one reign or period of supreme government
> by one person, as well as detached laws and
> documents separately enacted and issued, to be
> catalogued under the name of the person in whose
> name or by whose authority they are enacted or
> sanctioned; such names to be entered alphabetically
> under the principal entry of the state or nation,
> after the general collections . . .

The wording of the first rule makes it clear that corporate authorship only applies to publications whose content has been agreed on by the corporate body as a whole, though later editions of the code modify this to some extent. The second rule quoted clearly establishes the principle of regarding governments as the authors of their official publications, including laws, and differs little from subsequent codes'

1 Yvonne Ruyssen, and Suzanne Honore. Corporate authors and the cataloguing of of official publications. *Journal of documentation* 13 (3) 132-146.
2 Julia Pettee. *op cit.*

treatment of the same type of material. These two rules, taken together, appear to indicate the British Museum's acceptance of the principle that corporate bodies (including governments) should be considered authors of publications reflecting their corporate views. The interpretation of Ruyssen and Honore that this merely amounts to a regrouping of basically anonymous publications under a geographical heading would not seem to be borne out by a close examination of the rules quoted above. This seems far removed from the subsequent German treatment of corporate publications as anonymous if no personal name appears on the title-page. The publications of corporate bodies represent a large mass of material which must be organized in some fashion. The German solution is dispersal throughout the catalogue. Another solution would be form entry, but even with this solution there would still be the problem of subarrangement under the form heading so that in the end it would be difficult to avoid entry under names of corporate bodies. As we shall see later, the British Museum does employ this solution for certain specified types of corporate body — academies and learned societies. This solution was, however, abandoned between the first and second editions of the General Catalogue of Printed Books, as we shall notice later. Panizzi and his 91 rules laid the foundation on which later codes were to develop the intellectual responsibility concept as applied to the publications of corporate bodies. In the 1936 edition of the rules, rule 16 makes it reasonably clear that, with the exception of learned institutions, a corporate body acting merely in a publishing capacity is not to be taken for entry.

While Panizzi in 1841 accepted the validity of corporate authorship, he also recognised the difficulties which ensues once corporate authorship is accepted. These difficulties are chiefly concerned with the form of entry for corporate bodies, and Panizzi foresaw the difficulties presented by the names of corporate bodies. This is why the 1841 rules quoted above do not enter corporate bodies directly under their names, but under the name of the country or place from which they derive their names, or in the absence of such a name, under the name of the place where they are located, thus avoiding the difficulties of corporate bodies having common names. This consistent entry under a geographical name is modified in the 1936 edition of the rules, where entry under a geographical name is prescribed for all official bodies and also for non-official bodies of a national character, which would be entered under the name of the country (rule 5). Other types of non-official bodies, commercial firms, international organisations and religious orders are entered directly under their names. This is foreshadowed by rule LXXXIV in 1841:

Religious and military orders to be designated
by the English name under which they are
generally known, and entries to be made
accordingly.

The exception to the entry of corporate bodies under the name of the country or place occurs in rule LXXX which runs as follows:

All acts, memoirs, transactions, journals, minutes,
etc. of academies, institutes, associations,
universities, or societies learned, scientific, or
literary, by whatever name known or designated,
as well as works by various hands, forming part of
a series of volumes edited by any such society,
to be catalogued under the general name "Academies"
and alphabetically entered under the English name
of the country and town at which the sittings of the
society are held, in the following order . . .

The entries under Academies are to be under the name of the continent, country, place, and then by the name of the body; each group being in alphabetical order. This is patently form rather than author entry, and may have been occasioned by the lack of distinctive names for these learned bodies, especially on the continent of Europe, and because their names are liable to frequent alteration. The form heading 'Academies' is in line with similar headings to be found in the British Museum catalogue — Periodical Publications, Ephemerides, Almanacs, Catalogues and Encyclopaedias. By employing these form headings, Panizzi was by no means unique, but merely following a fairly common contemporary practice. By 1841, the concept of authorship as the determinant of all the headings in the
28

author catalogue had not developed. The British Museum rules have, however, tended to accept the more rigorous application of the concept of authorship based on intellectual responsibility, and through the years the number of these form headings for certain classes of material has diminished. The heading 'Academies' does not appear in the second edition of the *General catalogue,* the entries being dispersed under the names of places or the names of the bodies themselves. This process of abandoning form headings seems likely to continue![1]

Two minor exceptions to the principle of entry under author first appeared in the British Museum rules of 1841, and have been repeated in most subsequent codes. They occur in rule XXXVII, and are given in italics, indicating the additional rules found necessary when the work on the catalogue was under way. The rules are:

In criminal proceedings the name of the defendant to be adopted as a heading.

Trials relating to any vessel to be entered under the name of such vessel.

This is neither form nor author entry, but entry according to the name most prominent on a title-page or most permanently associated with a work.

In summary, it may be said that, while Panizzi's code of 1841 is the obvious ancestor of all later codes, he often preferred the direct to the indirect catalogue, and entered certain classes of works under the most obvious heading rather than under a heading which was more closely derived from principles of authorship and intellectual responsibility. These principles were to be developed later by men like Cutter and the editors of AA(1908). Whether their or Panizzi's approach was more correct is a debateable point, as many of Panizzi's headings have come back into favour in recent years, *vide* Lubetzky and CCR (1960). One surprising element of the British Museum code is its modernity. It has stood the test of time well, and bears comparison with, for example, CCR (1960) constructed over one hundred years later. Panizzi's insistence on the use of title-page information for the derivation of headings is essentially modern. The timelessness of Panizzi's rules is perhaps the

1   Mary Piggott, *ed.*Cataloguing principles and practice: and inquiry. London, 1954.

greatest tribute to his achievement.

3
CHARLES COFFIN JEWETT

After the publication of the British Museum rules in 1841, the
initiative passed to the other side of the Atlantic, and rested,
in 1852,,in Charles C Jewett, then Librarian of the Smithsonian
Institution in Washington, with the publication of *The
Smithsonian report on the construction of catalogues of libraries,
and their publication by means of separate stereo-titles, with
rules and examples.* A second edition appeared in *1853.* The
primary purpose of the publication was, of course, to arouse
interest in a form of centralised cataloguing. Briefly, Jewett's
proposals were that the Smithsonian Institution would print
stereotype entries for a printed book catalogue. The stereotype
blocks would be stored at the Smithsonian, and could be used
to print catalogues of other libraries. Thus the heaviest cost of
printing, that of typesetting, would be avoided, and uniformity
would also be obtained. Libraries were to contribute manuscript
entries for stereotyping if the stereotype blocks did not already
exist at the Smithsonian. Thus it was obvious that an agreed
code of cataloguing rules would be essential to the scheme.
Hence the existence of the rules given as the second part of the
Report. In general Jewett accepted most of Panizzi's rules,
with some minor modifications, and at least one major
difference.

Like Panizzi before him, Jewett made no attempt to define
authorship, though, as in the earliest set of rules, many of his
rules codify situations where there may be a choice between
different names for author entry. With some few exceptions,
Jewett continued the work of Panizzi and laid the foundation
for the later Anglo-American concept of authorship based
upon the principle of intellectual responsibility.
31

Rules for the choice of heading follow twelve rules relating to the transcription of titles, where the emphasis is laid on the need to repeat the author's name in the title-transcript, a practice not followed in the British Museum, but repeated in AA (1908) and ALA (1949). Jewett had to insist on this repetition, not because of any insistence on bibliographical completeness in the entries, but because the titles were to be stereotyped separately from the headings. One may wonder if the editors of the later codes had such practical reasons for the repetition of authors' names in titles as did Jewett. The point of constructing unit entries from title transcripts, without main author headings will be discussed later when future developments are considered.

Rule XIII states that, after the title has been transcribed according to the previous twelve rules, the heading is to be written above it. The extent that Jewett separated rules for title from those of heading also makes him modern, and in line with CCR (1960) and AACR (1967). In general the heading consists of the name of the author in its vernacular form, when this can be represented by letters of the English alphabet. No attempt is made to define authorship. To Jewett and Panizzi it would seem that problems of authorship did not exist. The problems of under whom to enter are dealt with in rules XX to XXIX, and on the whole follow Panizzi rather closely.

Joint authorship (rule XX) is rather ambiguously defined and treated − 'If it appear on the title-page that the work is a joint production of several writers, it is to be entered under the first named, with cross-references from the names of the others.' From the rule and the example given by Jewett it is not clear whether he is referring to joint or composite authorship, or more likely, both.

COBBETT (William)
Elements of the Roman history, in English and French, from the foundation of Rome to the battle of Actium; selected from the best authors, ancient and modern, with a series of questions... The English by William Cobbett; the French by J.H.Sievrac.
London, 1828. 12º (5.5 x 3.1) [1029]
Note − With title-page in French.

Panizzi would have preferred entry under both authors, if, as
is not clear from the transcript, the work is not a translation
from the French of Jean Henri Sievrac. The distinction between
joint and composite authorship is made even less clear by the
following rule for collections (rule XXI):

> The complete works, or entire treatises of
> several authors, published together in one
> series, with a collective title, are to be
> recorded in the words of the general title
> of the series, and to be placed under the
> name of the editor, if known; if that be
> not known, under the title of the collection,
> like anonymous works.

Example

> GALE (Thomas)
>> Historiae poeticae scriptores antiqui. Apollodorus
>> Atheniensis. Conon Grammaticus. Ptolomaeus
>> Hephaest. f.   . . .
>>> *Parisius,* 1675.8⁰ (5.5 x 3.3) 3 pagings
>>> [1002]

The later subtle distinctions between joint and collective
authorship recognised by AA (1908) had not yet developed, and
Jewett also made the point clear that for him collective
authorship only applied to the complete works of an author, when
brought together with the complete works of another author or
authors. In an explanation of rule XXI, Jewett indicates that it
also applies to periodicals:

> This rule applies to periodical publications,
> which should be entered under the name of the
> Editor, if this appears on the title-page, with a
> cross-reference from the name of the publication.

Example

> BELL (Thomas), *sec. R.S.*
>> The zoological journal. V. 1,2 From March,
>> 1824 . . . to April, 1826. Conducted by
>> Thomas Bell, esq., F.L.S. . . . V.3, 4. From
>> January, 1827 . . . to May, 1829. Edited by
>> N.A. Vigors, . . . [*with plates*]
>>> *London,* 1825 − '29. 8⁰ (6.2 x 3.6) [2940]

No reference is indicated from the title of the periodical in
33

Jewett's series of examples with supporting references which he supplies at the end of his code. This form of entry would appear to be cataloguing by any personal name appearing on a title-page. It is obvious from the transcript that the editorial responsibility of Mr Thomas Bell was limited to the first two volumes. Nor does Mr Vigors receive any reference in the list of examples. If, however, the publication is issued under the direction of an association, it would be catalogued according to the following rules, and is entered under the name of the association.

This brings us to rule XXII, the rule establishing corporate authorship. While Panizzi was willing to recognise the validity of the principle of corporate authorship, he was less willing to accept entry of corporate bodies under their names as they stood, preferring entry under country or place, and reserving name entry for a relatively small section of corporate authors. Miss Pettee states 'Jewett's rule XXII is a sweeping innovation extending the principle of authorship entry to all corporate bodies.[1]

The rule runs as follows:-
Academies, institutions, associations,
universities, colleges; literary, scientific,
economical, eleemosynary and religious societies;
national and municipal governments; assemblies,
conventions, boards, corporations, and other
bodies of men under whatever name, and of
whatever character, issuing publications, whether
as separate works, or in a continuous series,
under a general title, are to be considered and
treated as the authors of all works issued by
them, and in their name alone. The heading is to
be the name of the body, the principal word to be
the first word, not an article. A cross reference
is to be made from any important substantive or
adjective, to the principal word.

Jewett prefers direct entry under the name of the body to entry either under a catch-word in the title of the body, or some substitute for the name of the body, *eg* place or country. Again, to this extent Jewett is modern. Lubetzky returned to this

1 Julia Pettee. *op cit*, p 282

position in 1953 after cataloguers had for so long remained in the wilderness of the distinction between societies and institutions introduced by AA (1908). Jewett seemed to have no qualms that direct entry under the first word of the name of the body would result in accumulations of entries in the catalogue under common words like University, etc.

Jewett's next rule (rule XXIII) deals with translations, and clearly states that translations are to be entered under the heading for the original work, an obvious example of the operation of the intellectual responsibility concept. He makes this doubly clear when he states 'If the name of the translator be known, and that of the author unknown, the book is to be entered, like other anonymous works, under the first word of the original title . . ., whether the original be or be not in the library to be catalogued.' This was a point which Jewett's successors, who framed AA (1908) failed to appreciate and introduced inconsistencies, as will be discussed later when AA (1908) is reviewed.

Jewett's rule for Pseudonyms (rule XXVIII) is rather similar to Panizzi's, though differing in one important respect. Both accept pseudonyms (assumed names) as headings, even if the real name of the author is known, but Panizzi would treat each edition or copy of a book on its own merits, where Jewett would not treat as pseudonymous any work of which any edition, continuation, or supplement had been issued under the author's real name. Neither set of rules makes any attempt to observe the literary unit, though in Jewett's rule can be seen observance of the bibliographical unit. Also in accord with Panizzi's code, Jewett would enter works where the author's name is represented only by initials under the initials, again, unless the author is known to have published any edition under his full name.

Jewett and Panizzi did not agree over anonymous works (rule XXIX). Panizzi favoured entry under the most prominent word in the title and provided a set of rules for the choice of such a word. Jewett established entry of anonymous works under the first word of the title not an article *or a preposition.* First word entry for anonymous works has been a feature of Anglo-American cataloguing, with the exception of the British Museum, from Jewett to the present day. Jewett makes clear that an anonymous work is one in which the author's names does not appear at all in the book itself. Again, if the author published any edition, continuation or supplement to the work under his name, it would not be regarded as anonymous. Jewett's exception is for an anonymous biography or personal narrative, which is to be entered under the name of the person who is the subject of the book, *if the name appears on the title-page.* This, of course, is subject entry in the author catalogue, and is based on no principle of author cataloguing. It is perhaps a survival of Panizzi's rule of entry for anonymous works under the most prominent word in the title; a personal name in the title being given priority of choice by Panizzi. This particular deviation from author cataloguing is also followed by Cutter.

Summary of Jewett's contribution
So far as his scheme for a form of co-operative/centralised cataloguing went, Jewett's proposals did not bear fruit, and in this respect his work failed, like many other schemes which were too far in advance of contemporary thought and practice. Perhaps Jewett underestimated the practical and technical difficulties, particularly those of storing large numbers of stereotype plates. In the event, little more was heard of his scheme. In 1855, the American Antiquarian Society postponed the publication of its catalogue for two or three years in the hope that by that time Jewett's plan would be realised![1] Jewett severed his connection with the Smithsonian in 1854, loser of the struggle to make it a national library and this fact, coupled with the difficulties of the material Jewett chose for his stereotype plates, may account for the failure of his schemes. In 1855, Jewett became librarian of Boston Public Library, where, like many of his contemporaries, he turned his energies towards the production of catalogues. His catalogues at Boston were greatly admired in their time, their main interest being in their treatment of subject entries. Jewett, in his code of rules for the Smithsonian was little of an innovator, taking most of his inspiration from the work of Panizzi, but he did much to formalise and introduce into the American continent English concepts of cataloguing. This introduction was sub-

1 Jim Ranz. The printed book catalogue in American libraries, 1723-1900 (ACRL monograph no 26), 1964, pp 47-48.

sequently to bear fruit in the work of Charles Ammi Cutter at the Boston Athenaeum. The initiative in cataloguing principles and practice was to remain on the Western side of the Atlantic Ocean for the remainder of the nineteenth century.

4
CUTTER'S RULES FOR A DICTIONARY CATALOGUE

The first edition of Charles Ammi Cutter's *Rules for a dictionary catalogue* was published in 1876, and the fourth and last edition was published a year after Cutter's death in 1903. They have been reprinted many times since, and constitute the best-selling book on any aspect of librarianship. The *Rules* were the culmination of a lifelong experience of librarianship and cataloguing in the United States. Cutter's code, while being an eminently practical code, is nevertheless the first code of cataloguing rules to be based on stated principles of The principles laid down by Cutter in 1876 remained almost without challenge until almost the present decade — a testimony to their value. Unlike the other codes under consideration in this paper, Cutter's rules deal not only with author and title entries, but also with all other types of entry to be found in the dictionary catalogue, as their title indicates. Subject entries are outwith the scope of the present paper; suffice to say that the dictionary catalogue as finalised by Cutter has undergone remarkably little change since. Cutter's work summated that of his predecessors, at least on the American continent, and also formed the basis of most author cataloguing for the first half of the twentieth century. This may be illustrated by the 'Objects' of a dictionary catalogue which Cutter sets out in detail.[1]

  1 To enable a person to find a book of which either
    (A) The author   )
    (B) The title   )   is known
    (C) The subject)
  2 To show what the library has

1 C A Cutter. Rules for a dictionary catalog; 4th ed, 1904, p 12.

38

    (D) By a given author
    (E) On a given subject
    (F) In a given kind of literature
 3 To assist in the choice of a book
    (G) As to its edition (bibliographically)
    (H) As to its character (literary or topical).

These 'Objects' may be compared, insofar as author and title
entries are concerned, with an almost identical set of principles
stated in the ICCP Principles of Paris in 1961.[1] Elsewhere, on
page 31, in an introduction to the section of the rules dealing
with choice of author, Cutter states that the object of author
entry:

> Is not merely to facilitate the finding of a
> given book by the author's name. If this were
> all, it might have been better to make the
> entry, as proposed by Mr.Crestadoro, under the
> part of the name mentioned in the title (which
> would have Bulwer in one book, Lytton in another,
> Bulwer Lytton in a third...) or under the name of
> editor or translator when the author's name is
> not given. This might have been best with object
> A; but we also have object D to provide for — the
> finding of all books of a given author— and this
> can most conveniently be done if all are collected
> in one place.

Cutter's definition of authorship places his rules firmly with
the intellectual responsibility concept; indeed, it might be said
that Cutter, more than anyone, was responsible for the concept.
In Cutter's rules we find the first statement of the concept,
which was later accepted almost without alteration by AA
(1908) and also ALA (1949):

> *Author,* In the narrower sense, is the person who
> writes a book; in a wider sense it may be applied
> to him who is the cause of the book's existence
> by putting together the writings of several
> authors (usually called *the editor,* more properly
> to be called *the collector).* Bodies of men (societies,
> cities, legislative bodies, countries) are to be considered the

1 International Conference on Cataloguing Principles, Paris, 9th-18th October
    1961, London, 1963. p 28, Structure of the catalogue.

authors of their memoirs, transactions,
journals, debates, reports, etc.

This definition may be compared with that given in AA (1908) to establish their similarity.[1]

The first part of the definition is the classical definition of the intellectual responsibility concept, but to extend the definition to that of collectorship or editorship would base authorship on an entirely different principle. Cutter himself would seem to have his doubts, and only be prepared to extend his definition to collectorship, and not to editorship. But even a collector of other people's writings, while having responsibility for a particular collection can hardly be said to be responsible for their contributions. The same contributions may appear in other collections under other editors. To include collectorship within the definition of authorship would seem to confuse the 'book' with the 'work'. Cutter's Objects stated above clearly indicate that he is interested in cataloguing the 'work' rather than the 'book', but in his definition of author he is confusing the two. It may be that a definition of author based on the intellectual responsibility concept may be inadequate to explain all the types of entry found in Cutter's code. If this is so, and it manifestly is, then the solution is not to extend authorship into editorship and collectorship, but to provide a definition of a different species of authorship.

As in AA (1908), the first section of Cutter's rules is the one which concerns us most, *ie* A, Where to enter, rules 1 to 22 and 45 to 95. Rules 1 to 22 in Cutter's code are almost exactly parallel to the first twenty-two rules in AA (1908) dealing with the same problem (Under whom as author?). The parallel is too close to be accidental, and indicates the genesis of this section of AA (1908). AA (1908) will be considered in more detail later, and as the rules in the two codes more or less agree, only the main points of difference will be commented on here. One important difference is the inclusion of a rule for anonymous works by Cutter (rule 2), whereas this is dealt with under rules for title entry in AA (1908). True to his objective D, Cutter would enter anonymous works under the names of their authors when known, and if not, under the name of the person to whom the work is attributed

1 Cataloguing rules: author and title entries, 1908, p xvii.

40

(the latter is ignored in the AA (1908) code). If the anonymous work is not attributed to anyone, entry is to be made under the title of the work. It is more logical to include the rule for anonymous works in the section on authorship, as it is after all a negative condition of authorship, than to include the rule under title entry as in AA (1908).

Multiple authorship
In the case of multiple authorship, Cutter introduces some rules and principles which were not followed by his immediate successors. In short, Cutter does not appear to recognise joint authorship as it is defined in AA (1908) and subsequent codes, as the writing of a book in conjunction with one or more authors, the parts written by each not usually being specified. Cutter, it is true, has a definition of joint authorship as:

Writing a book in conjunction *with* specification
of the part written by each.[1]

Such conditions of multiple authorship Cutter would enter, according to rule 3, under the name of the first author appearing on the title-page, with references from the others. This would include writers of a correspondence and participants in a debate. Cutter states his reason for entry under the first author only in rule 218, because such a heading, consisting of one name only, leads to better arrangement in the catalogue. This is Cutter's rejoinder to the AA (1908) code's entry of works of joint authorship by two authors under a joint heading consisting of both of their names. It is significant that the Library of Congress in its printed cards scheme, which started in 1901, has consistently followed Cutter's practice of single name headings for joint authorship.

The other type of undifferentiated multiple authorship recognised by Cutter is collections, *ie* the bringing together of several works or parts of works, which, by rule 98, would be entered under the collector, provided they have been published with a collective title. This is covered by Cutter's extended definition of authorship already alluded to. Cutter's position would thus seem to be that he recognised a distinction between joint authorship — the bringing together of new contributions under one volume, and collections — the collection of previously

1. C A Cutter, *op cit,* p 21.
41

existing works, generally under an editor and collective title. This is more or less the distinction between composite and collective works as maintained in ALA (1949). Joint authorship, as defined in later codes, Cutter ignores altogether.

Differentiated multiple authorship
The remainder of the first twenty two rules in Cutter's code deal with the problem of what later came to be known as differentiated multiple authorship, *ie* where two or more persons perform different functions in relation to a work, such as author and editor, translator, illustrator, etc. Cutter's rules covering these problems are concerned largely with the application of the intellectual responsibility principle. The exceptions will be noted later. Illustrated works (rule 8) caused him some trouble, as it did later codes as well. The principle of intellectual responsibility would result in cataloguing under the person who was primarily responsible for the publication, writer or artist. In cases where the illustrations are as important as, or even more important than the text, Cutter and most later codes get into some difficulty. Cutter's rule runs as follows:

When the illustrations form a very important part
of a work, consider both the author of the text and
the designer — or in certain cases the engraver —
of the plates to be author, and make a full entry
under each. Under the author mention the designer's
name in the title, and vice versa.

In a card catalogue the entry under the writer of the text is to be considered the main entry, presumably in all circumstances. This resource to double entry is employed in a number of instances in this section of Cutter's rules. While such an expedient may be satisfactory for a book catalogue, it is not very successful for a card catalogue, where one entry must always be designated the main entry, so that the tracings of the other entries can be written on the back of the card, nor is it satisfactory in single-entry catalogues such as union catalogues. The first difficulty Cutter surmounts by nominating the entry under the writer as the main entry. This is not ascribing intellectual responsibility but merely indicating which card will bear the tracings. The other problem Cutter ignores completely.

However, in rule 9, primary responsibility for a work is
42

Cutter's guiding factor, where a designer or painter copied, a cartographer, an engraver (of a collection of engravings) and an architect are to be considered as authors of books of drawings, maps, plans, etc produced by them. Photographers are not so treated in the following rules. In the case of a collection of photographs taken by them, they need not in general have an entry, even in a special catalogue of photographs. Presumably the camera to Cutter is a mere mechanical recording instrument incapable of interpreting the user's thoughts or personality, a point of view doubtlessly nor shared by modern photographers (or cataloguers).

Vocal music presents a similar problem to graphic works with text. Cutter again applies his solution of double entry. He also avoids, in the absence of a specific rule on the subject, the problem of how to deal with librettos, *ie* the separate publication of the words of operas, etc. In the absence of a specific rule, Cutter would presumably enter under the author of the words in the case of a separately published libretto.

Cutter's rule 13 would appear to ignore entirely the intellectual principle of authorship when it states that auctioneers' catalogues of a public library, gallery or museum should be catalogued under the name of the library, gallery or museum, and of a private library, etc under the name of the owner, unless there is reason to believe another person made it. Why should only auctioneers' catalogues be treated in this manner? Other official catalogues are not mentioned, but these would presumably also be entered under the name of the library, museum, etc. whose contents they list. Intellectual responsibility would presumably dictate entry under the name of the compiler of the catalogue, though this could be open to the same objection as entering a collection under the compiler. Entry under owner can only be based on the name most prominently associated with a work, on the assumption that previous catalogues have been compiled by different auctioneers in the past, and could also be so compiled in the future. Entry under the name of the owning body or person is tantamount to subject entry.

In rule 16, Cutter again employs the double entry principle for the determination of the main entry in the case of indexes and continuations of previously existing works. When printed with the original, these are to be entered under the heading for

43

the original work; if not, they are to be entered under each author. In the first case one could hardly do otherwise, and in the second, Cutter has fallen back on his double entry principle, thus leaving the choice of main entry completely open. He follows the same principle for concordances in rule 20:

> Enter concordances both under their own author
> and the author concorded. The latter entry, however,
> is to be regarded as a subject entry.

The last provision, while it may be adequate for a dictionary catalogue, is of little help in cataloguing for an author catalogue. This was one of the rules in which the national committees could not agree in drawing up AA (1908). The American edition agrees with Cutter in entering a concordance under its compiler. To enter under the author concorded is virtually subject entry, as Cutter himself says. Entry under the author concorded in an author catalogue is cataloguing according to the name most prominently and permanently associated with a work.

In summary, Cutter bases his rules for personal authorship broadly on the intellectual responsibility concept, but is forced on occasion to reserve judgement and enter doubly in the case of vocal works, illustrated works, indexes, supplements, and concordances, and to abandon the principle altogether in the case of auctioneers' catalogues, and adopt that of the name most prominently associated with the work.

Corporate authorship
Outwith the section in Cutter's code 'Under whom as author', which covers personal authors only, is the section on corporate authorship. While corporate authorship had been recognised as a valid type of authorship by Panizzi in 1841, he showed considerable reluctance to use the names of corporate bodies as headings. Later codes showed a similar reluctance. Names of corporate bodies provide numerous problems and pitfalls for the compiler of a code of cataloguing rules – they change, they are often not distinctive, and so on. This was presumably why Panizzi favoured entry under country or place for most cate-gories of corporate body. Jewett was in favour of name entry, as was the Bodleian, but Cutter firmly established in Algo-American cataloguing practice, entry under the name of the
44

corporate body as first choice. On page 40 of the fourth edition of his rules Cutter states the case for corporate authorship.

> Before the 'Rules for a dictionary catalog' were made catalogs seemed to me to be chaotic collections of empirical entries. I tried to find a few simple principles around which all desirable practices could be grouped. One of these principles is corporate authorship and editorship. I have as yet seen nothing to convince me that it is not a good one, since it corresponds to fact, inasmuch as societies are the authors of their proceedings and the collectors of their series . . .

Cutter's defence of corporate authorship is largely in the face of the German practice of regarding all such publications as anonymous, and entering under the first independent noun in their titles. The principles laid down by Cutter in 1876 have been modified in detail by later codes, but in substance they have altered little. His rules were, however, drawn up in 1876, when corporate authorship had neither achieved the proportions nor the variety which it has assumed in later years. Cutter states his basic rule in rule 45:

> Bodies of men are to be considered as authors of works published in their name or by their authority.

In a note appended to the rule he enumerates the main problems:

> The chief difficulty with regard to bodies of men is to determine (1) what their names are, and (2) whether the name or some other word shall be the heading.

The difficulties over names does not concern us here, but the statement 'in their name or by their authority' is of concern. 'In their name' presumably means that the corporate body is prepared to accept responsibility for the views and statements expressed in the publication, even if it is not actually the author. This would obviously cover administrative reports, which are normally written by an officer of the body, but also have to have the sanction of the body as a whole.'The subject matter is the responsibility of the body as a whole, and the name of the mane who chances to sign the report is of no consequence'.[1] This is reasonably consistent with the intellectual responsibility

1. L Jolley. Principles of cataloguing, London, 1961, p 58.

concept. The corporate body, while not responsible for the actual composition or writing of the document, is prepared to accept responsibility for the views expressed therein. Someone must write such a report. So Cutter would appear to include here normal routine reports setting out the views and activities of a corporate body.

'By their authority' would seem to suggest a less definite connection between the body and the publication, which does not necessarily imply intellectual responsibility for the contents of the publication. Many of the publications of the Royal Institute of International Affairs, for example, are issued under their authority, but the Institute expressly disclaims any responsibility for the views expressed therein. This problem does not appear to have been envisaged by Cutter. It is the problem of personal *vs* corporate name on title-pages, a problem nowhere touched upon by Cutter. Yet it is one of the most difficult cataloguing problems to solve, and one where the only criterion must be the intellectual responsibility yardstick. In this situation, phrases like 'published in the name of', or 'by the authority of' a corporate body do not always help one to decide between the two types of authorship. Presumably any corporate body which is willing to allow its name to appear on the title-page of a publication would at least concur with the views expressed in the work, although this may not necessarily be so, as instanced by the Royal Institute of International Affairs above. Such a situation does not amount to authorship. As an example we may consider the series of works on the press, film and radio issued by Unesco, or the various series issued in this country by the Ministry of Agriculture. These are issued by the authority of the respective corporate bodies, but the bodies do not claim intellectual responsibility for them, or the views expressed therein. The documents represent the views of experts invited by the corporate bodies to contribute. Both represent distinct series, and one has the feeling that because their series.' Cutter would enter them collectively under the name of the corporate body. This is confirmed by the statement of Cutter's already quoted — 'Societies are authors of their proceedings and collectors of their series.' The phrase 'collectors of their series' would seem to suggest an entirely different criterion of authorship,

46

namely, the name most permanently associated with a work or series of works. In many instances the corporate body may only function as publisher, and entry under its name is tantamount to entry under publisher. Current practice favours the personal name, and regards the case for corporate entry as having to be proved.

Cutter would thus appear to confine corporate authorship to those cases where no personal name appears on a title-page, *ie* regular transactions, reports, journals, etc of a corporate body, and those publications of corporate bodies issued in series, *ie* where the name of the corporate body is the only one printed on the title-page, and the only alternative to corporate entry is entry under title. His introductory discussion of corporate authorship would seem to confirm this view.[1] In other words, Cutter accepts corporate entry as a substitute for anonymous entry under the first word of the title; he does not consider it in relation to personal author entry, when both personal and corporate names appear on a title-page. It may be, of course, that in such circumstances, Cutter would always choose personal authorship, but he does not specifically say so. Corporate authorship is not based on the intellectual responsibility criterion, but is merely a concept of convenience useful to avoid entry under title.

Cutter's contribution to the theory of author cataloguing was considerable. His code was the first to be based on principles, and because these principles were firmly rooted in practical experience, they have stood the test of time, and formed the basis of most author cataloguing theory for the next hundred years.

1 C A Cutter. Rules for a dictionary catalog; 4th ed, 1904. pp 39-41.

5
THE ANGLO-AMERICAN CODE, 1908

Cataloguing rules: author and title entries, 1908 represented an early example of co-operation, in this instance between the (British) Library Association and the American Library Association. The co-operation was first suggested by Melvil Dewey, when he discovered that both associations were engaged on the revision of their existing rules. The Americans were revising their rules of 1883 to bring them into line with the practice of the Library of Congress in its printed card service, which started in January, 1901. They were also anxious to reach accord with the fourth edition of Cutter's rules (1904). The Library Association were revising their rules, also of 1883. The interest of the Americans in Library of Congress practice emphasises the fact that they were designing a set of rules primarily for a card catalogue, while in this country we were still in favour of the printed bóok form of catalogue. The adoption of the card catalogue by libraries in this country lagged behind that of the United States. Indeed, the first decade of the present century in this country marked the high water-mark of the printed book catalogue, with the completion of the monumental British Museum Catalogue.[1] We were still in the era of the printed book catalogue while the Americans were moving away from it. Any attempt to reconcile the rules for these two types of catalogue was bound to be a difficult operation, and it is to the credit of the two committees that so little disagreement resulted. In only eight of the one hundred and seventy four rules did they disagree, and in half of the cases the disagreement concerned change of name or form of heading. The British, with their eyes on the needs of the printed book

1   British Museum.General catalogue of printed books, 1881-1900. 95v, *and* Supplement, 1900-1905, 13v.

catalogue were naturally in favour of the earliest form of name; while the Americans, exploring the greater flexibility of the card catalogue, were more generally in favour of the later or more current forms.

AA (1908) has had a long currency in this country, remaining the official code for fifty nine years, until the publication of the recent *Anglo American cataloguing rules, 1967.* These fifty nine years have seen the ascendancy of the card catalogue, but our rules have been based largely on the peculiar needs of the printed book form of catalogue.

The basic design and objectives of the AA (1908) code
In the first place, the code is limited to rules for author and title cataloguing, and for the description of books and other documents. Generally, entry is under author, and in the absence of author, under title. AA (1908) is specifically designed for the needs of the large collection, unlike Cutter's Long, Medium and Short cataloguing. The rules are also based on the practice of giving as many entries in the catalogue for a work as are necessary for its retrieval, the primary entry being regarded as the Main entry, and the others are Added entries. This entails the use of unit entries in the case of the card catalogue, but rather of references in the case of the printed book catalogue. Hence the frequence existence with many of the rules of a choice between these two forms of accommodating other approaches to the work in the catalogue than by the main entry. The corollary is that the British would prefer references, and the Americans added entries.

AA (1908) firmly adheres to the literary unit concept of author and title cataloguing, but generally ignores the concept of the bibliographic unit. This can be seen in the rule for translations (rule 21) which merely states that translations are to be entered under the heading of the original work, ignoring completely the problem of which title to use. AA (1908) also accepts the concept of intellectual responsibility as the main determinant of the author heading, but, as we shall see later, this does not always prove adequate for solving all problems of authorship. The application of this and the previous principle occasionally results in entries under headings which would be extremely difficult for the uninitiated to find in the
49

catalogue, even having the work in question open in front of them. When AA (1908) deems the intellectual responsibility concept to be inadequate as the determinant of an author heading, it falls back on other criteria, for example, the name most permanently or prominently identified with a work, the concept of the subordinate work, and occasionally form entry.

The arrangement of the rules in AA (1908) is not particularly successful. They are generally arranged into groups according to the heading or form of heading which the application of a particular rule would achieve. This results in the unfortunate scattering of rules dealing with related problems, for example that of the multi-author book, and the general problem of unknown or disguised authorship.

AA (1908) also adopts an enumerative approach to cataloguing rules, attempting to provide a rule for every problem. As the varieties of problems and authorship were not so numerous in 1908 as they have subsequently become, the code has become more and more inadequate to deal with new forms of authorship. This particular inadequacy has been aggravated by the code's attention to the problems presented by specific types of publication and its lack of attention to the conditions lying behind the problems, and to the occasional exceptions to general rules for particular types of publication or form of name. Very few general principles can be deduced from a mass of 'ad hoc' rules covering specific decisions.

Definition of authorship in AA (1908)
AA (1908) usefully contains a list of definitions of terms as used in the code. Author is defined as:
> 1. The writer of a book, as distinguished from translator, editor, etc. etc. 2. In a broader sense, the maker of the book or the person or body immediately responsible for its existence. Thus, a person who collects and puts together the writings of several authors (compiler or editor) may be said to be the author of a collection. Corporate bodies may be considered the authors of publications issued in their name or by their authority.

This definition closely resembles Cutter's quoted on page 39, though the definition of a corporate author in AA (1908) is a bit looser than that given by Cutter. It is perhaps significant that in neither definition do the words 'On the title-page' appear. The first part of the definition clearly subscribes to the intellectual responsibility concept; the second part of the definition extending authorship to editorship and collectorship is open to the objections already stated against Cutter's definition. This point will be taken up later when dealing with the problems of collective authorship in AA (1908).

The sections of AA (1908) which particularly appertain to our discussion are the following:

1. Under whom as author (rules 1-22).

2. Sections of corporate authorship — Governments, laws, societies and institutions (rules 58-111)

3. Title entry, particularly anonymous works (rules 112-129)

4. Miscellaneous headings (rules 130-135).

Personal authors — under whom as author
The main rule is quite straightforward (rule 1):
Enter a work under the name of its author,
whether individual or corporate.
A reference is made to the definition of authorship in the list of definitions already noted. The rule is given under Section a. *Personal authors,* but it covers more than this; corporate authorship is also included and exemplified. The rule should have been much more generalised and given as a basic rule for the whole code:
Enter a work under the name of its author, whether
individual or corporate, or some substitute for it,
or, in the absence of both of these elements, under the
first word of the title, not an article.
This, basically sums up the provisions of AA (1908).

The other rules in this section deal with situations where there is a choice of personal names for entry, arising from the following circumstances:

a. More than one person may perform the same function in the production of a work — Multiple authorship.

b. Different persons may perform different authorship functions in relation to a particular work; for example, writer of the text as opposed to the editor, illustrator, etc, composer of vocal music as opposed to the writer of the words; talker and reporter, etc — Differentiated multiple authorship.

Omissions from the section include: 1) substitute for author

51

when no personal name appears on a title page; 2) collections of works by various writers, which are dealt with in the section on title entry, but which are generally to be entered under the editor; 3) corporate authorship, which has a section to itself. The basic criterion in this section is intellectual responsibility. This can account for many of the rules. In fact, many of the rules are redundant, given this basic criterion. Other principles are: 1) name most permanently or prominently associated with a work; 2) the concept of the dependent work. The latter should be regarded as subordinate principles, and only used when the primary principle of intellectual responsibility is unsuitable. It will be a criticism of this section that, on occasion, these subordinate principles are introduced when the primary one would be quite adequate.

Multiple Authorship
The arrangement of the rules in AA (1908) is, as we have seen, not according to the cataloguing problem presented by certain types of work, but by the resultant form of heading achieved by the application of a given rule. This inevitably results in the separation of rules for similar problems. As an example, one could cite the separation of rules for unknown or disguised authorship, *ie* anonymous and pseudonymous works. The former, because they are entered under their titles, when the author is unknown, appear in the section on title entry, while the latter, being entered under the pseudonym when the author's real name is unknown, appear in the section entitled 'Under what part or form of name'. In this instance, the separation is particularly unfortunate because of the code's lack of a clear distinction between anonymous and pseudonymous authorship.

A similar separation occurs with works of multiple authorship. This covers the type of work, already defined, in which a number of persons have performed a similar authorship function, particularly joint authorship between collaborators, contributions by several authors, and all shades of variation between the two types. Joint authorship appears as rule 2 in the first section. Contributive or collective authorship appears as rule 126 under title entry. In multiple authorship it is almost impossible and certainly unwise to carry the intellectual basis

52

for authorship to its ultimate conclusion, if by this we would include in the heading a complete list of the contributors or collaborators to a volume. When there are more than two this would become impracticable in terms of filing the headings in an alphabetical catalogue. Like all codes AA (1908) acknowledges this difficulty by allowing two names in the heading, but no more, and recognising the presence of others by the suffix *and others* added to the first name.

If, as all codes agree, we cannot use all the names in the heading, a choice must be made, and the problem arises as to which name is to be chosen. Again, all codes agree on the choice of at least the first name appearing on the title-page. Presumably the first name is chosen as being the most prominent, and thus the name used by most enquiriers in seeking the work. Is this always a safe assumption? What if some name other than the first is considerably more important in contexts and works other than the one in hand? Is there a correlation between the order in which names are cited on title-pages of books and alphabetical order? Even if the choice of the first name on the title page could be justified, it is hardly intellectual responsibility that determines the heading, but the supposedly most prominent name on the title-page.

Joint authorship
AA (1908) defines a joint author as:
> A person who writes a book in collaboration with one or more associates, the portion written by each not usually being specified.

A product of joint authorship is to be distinguished from one of collective authorship, or contributive authorship, which by implication comprises works composed of separate contributions by several authors. Thus, if the parts written by each author are distinguishable, the work is to be treated as a collection, and not as a product of joint authorship, with one exception, correspondence, which is specifically included in rule 2 for joint authorship, though a volume of correspondence must obviously indicate the writer of each letter. Rule 2 itself does not make it completely clear whether only correspondence between *two* authors is included, or whether all correspondence is included. The next exact wording of the rule is as follows:
53

Enter a work written jointly by two authors (including correspondence) under the name of the one first mentioned on the title-page, followed by the name of the second, in the form, Besant, *Sir* Walter, *and* Rice, James. Where there are more than two authors use the form Doe, John, *and others;* give the names of the others in the title, if there are no more than three, or if more than three, in a note or in contents. Make added entries or references for the second and following authors.

The rule for collective authorship, *ie* including separate contributions by a number of authors is rule 126, which reads as follows:

Enter composite works and collections of independent works, essays, etc. by various authors under the compiler or editor, individual or corporate. If the work of the editor or editing body seems to be but slight and their names do not appear prominently in the publications, or if there are frequent changes of editor, enter under title.

The two rules cover similar types of material and authorship, and should be close together. Their separation by more than one hundred and twenty rules is by no means helpful. The distinction between the two rules is based on the distinction between the narrow and and broader definition of authorship already discussed. As we have noted before, the narrower definition of authorship is based on the intellectual responsibility concept, while the latter is based on the concept of responsibility for a particular collection. Even in rule 2 the intellectual responsibility concept is somewhat modified to produce a heading more amenable to filing than expressing complete intellectual responsibility for the work. This distinction between the two types of authorship as exemplified in the two rules is doubtfully tenable on theoretical grounds, and certainly not on practical ones. Without a survey of the nature of the contents of a work of multiple authorship the catalogue user has little means of deciding whether a number of names on a title-page represents joint or collective authorship, even assuming that he is aware of the different treatments accorded to the two types of authorship.

Nor does AA (1908) make any provision for subordinate joint authorship, if this is not a contradiction in terms. There is considerable argument for a ruling which would enter both joint and collective author ship under the name of the author who, by the typography or layout of the title-page is obviously meant to be regarded as the principal author, for example:
The British Patent System / 1. Administration/
K.H. Boehm. . . / In collaboration with Aubrey
Silberston . . ./ Cambridge University Press/
Silberston so obviously occupies a subordinate role in the partnership that it appears against the spirit of even AA(1908) to enter such a work jointly, though the contributions of each author may not be distinguishable. In both joint and contributive authorship there is every argument for entering under the name of a person responsible for the major part of a work.

ALA(1949) provides for this in rule 3B:
In a work of joint authorship in which the chief responsibility rests with one author, but the title-page reads 'with the collaboration of . . .' or words to that effect, the making of added entries for the collaborators will depend on (1) the nature of the work; (2) the number of collaborators and the importance of their contributions.

The inclusion of correspondence in AA (1908) rule for joint authorship is both interesting and confusing. Interesting because a volume of correspondence must show clearly the letters written by each correspondent, and therefore, this type of publication should not come within the definition of joint authorship, if we take the definition literally − 'The portion written by each not (usually) being specified.' Presumably the word 'usually' is there to cover correspondence. ALA (1949) defines 'joint author' as a person who collaborates with one or more associates to produce a work in which the contribution of each is not usually separable from that of the others. On this definition, corres-
55

pondence could conceivably be included within joint authorship. In the 1908 definition the words 'including correspondence' are only applied to works written jointly by two authors. There is no mention of correspondence later in the rule when three or more joint authors are dealt with. Are we to assume that correspondence between two letter writers is to be treated differently from that by more than two? If so, why?

As already noted, the other main rule for multiple authorship in AA (1908) is rule 126. The distinction between the type of material covered by the two rules, and the validity of the distinction has already been discussed. The result of rule 126 is to enter collective works under the names of their editors, provided the names appear on the title-pages, and the editors have done a reasonable amount of editing. The second second condition involves a subjective judgement on the part of the cataloguer, which should not be demanded of him. The choice of entry under editor or title should depend entirely on the occurence or non-occurence of the editor's name on the title-page. We have already discussed the point as to whether editorship of a collection is tantamount to intellectual responsibility, and we were doubtful if it was. An editor may be responsible for the form which a particular book takes, but he is no more intellectually responsible for the content of the contributions in multiple authorship than he is when he may edit the writings of one person. 'The compiler bears the responsibility for the collection of texts he has brought together, but cannot be regarded as responsible for the individual texts themselves'.[1] Under which principle can the rule be said to operate? It cannot be that of the name most prominent on the title-page. The editor's name may be given first, before the names of the contributors; on the other hand it may be given last, or even in the middle, if the editor is also a contributor.

The real solution lies in title entry. This would achieve consistency with the other rules in the same section of AA (1908) and would also save the cataloguer from having to decide whether the editorship is of sufficient quantity or quality to justify entry. The rule would then be consistent with those for similar types of material − dictionaries,

1   Helmut Braun. Multiple authorship. ICCP working paper no 10, 1963.

and encyclopaedias, yearbooks, directories, and other forms of contributive multiple authorship.

Whether to enter a collection under title or editor was a problem over which the Paris conference delegates were more evenly divided than over any other principle. Title entry won the day, but only with a substantial minority of the delegates supporting the alternative solution of entry under editor, if the amount of editing was adequate.[1]

An alternative solution is to abandon the distinction between co-operative and contributive authorship, and enter all examples of undifferentiated multiple authorship under the first author mentioned on the title-page , unqualified. This is the solution adopted by AA (1908) when the collection is published without a collective title, even though the name of an editor is given (rule 126^3). Why abandon editorship for main entry when it is so emphatically urged in the main rule? Rule 126^3 does not cater for the situation where the first work in a collection without a collective title may be anonymous and the author unknown, but obviously different from the author(s) of the other work(s) in the collection. The editor would be ignored altogether, and the extention of authorship into editorship in the definition could be avoided. The reasons for not adopting the name of the first author (or the title of the first work) in the collection as the heading are substantially the same as those which have already been put forward against first author entry in joint authorship, but they are more theoretically than practically important.

Differentiated multiple authorship
The second type of multiple authorship comprises those publications where the functions of the several persons named on the title-page are clearly defined, each acting in a different capacity in the production of the work. This type of authorship comprises the bulk of the rules in the first section of AA (1908) In this section the basic criterion for the choice of main entry heading is the intellectual responsibility concept, *ie* the name of the person to whom chief responsibility for the intellectual content of the work can be ascribed is taken as the heading. Assuming the operation of this criterion, many of the rules in

1   ICCP Report. Draft statement of principles, sections 10.2 & 10.3.

57

this section are redundant. Examples of such redundancy would be rules 13, Commentaries; 17, Epitomes; 18, Excerpts, chrestomathies; 20, Table-talk, interviews; and 21, Translations.

The concept of intellectual responsibility is, however, inadequate or inappropriate to solve all the problems of the choice of names for the heading. AA (1908) itself introduces others, namely the concept of the name most permanently associated with a work, and that of the dependent work. These other criteria may legitimately be used, but only in circumstances where the intellectual responsibility concept is inadequate or unsuitable. There are occasions when AA (1908) departs from the concept of intellectual responsibility without an adequate or obvious reason.

Rule 16 deals with concordances. It is the first of the eight instances where the two committees failed to agree. It is not surprising that the Americans failed to agree with their British colleagues when the latter chose to enter concordances under the author concorded, with merely an added entry under the compiler. The Americans correctly applied the intellectual responsibility concept here, and entered concordances under their compilers, regarding the entry under the author concorded as the subject entry. Cutter, as we have seen, evaded the problem, if there really is one, by using double entry. It is very difficult to defend the British rule in terms of the intellectual responsibility for a concordance. One can hardly ascribe intellectual responsibility to Shakespeare or Milton for an alphabetical list of the words used by them, which was compiled perhaps three centuries after their deaths. Any similarity to a selection from their works is merely superficial. To maintain that an alphabetical list of the words used by an author is similar to a selection from his writings is to deny the existence of literary style and even authorship itself. Authorship and style only become real when words are put together in a certain syntactical order. To enter under the author concorded is subject, nor author entry, as Cutter pointed out in his code. The British rule is based upon the criterion of 'name most permanently associated with a work', on the argument, pre- sumably, that if two or more concordances are compiled for one author's works the result will be more or less similar lists of words, and therefore these ought to go under the same heading in the catalogue. But alphabetical lists of words used in the English language would not be entered under 'English language', but under the names of their editors, as in rule 127 of AA (1908). To abandon the criterion of intellectual responsibility for concordances is to depart from a useful criterion in favour of one which leads to confusion of thought and practice.

The American committee, in rule 10, did not judge thematic catalogues to be similar to concordances. Both committees agreed to enter these under the original composer. Given that there is a close similarity between thematic catalogues and concordances, the American committee was to that extent inconsistent. But can a thematic catalogue be regarded as similar to a concordance? Are the themes used by a composer similar to the words used by an author? A closer parallel would be between the words used by an author and the notes used by a composer. Although the parallel is by no means complete, the entering of thematic catalogues under their composers still suggests the 'name most permanently associated with a work', rather than that of intellectual responsibility for the work as a *whole,* and also seems to have a touch of the subject entry about it. ALA (1949) reversed the rule (rule 12F):

Enter a thematic catalog under the compiler, if known, otherwise under the publisher. Make subject entry for the composer.

AA (1908) makes no provision for an added entry. If the name of the compiler is not known, presumably no entry would be required. In some instances the name of a compiler of a thematic catalogue is as well-known as that of the composer. Kochel and Mozart are perhaps the obvious examples.

The rule for *revisions* (rule 19) as stated in AA (1908) would appear to be a straightforward example of entry by intellectual responsibility:

Enter a revision under the name of the original author unless it has become substantially a new work, in which case it is to be entered under the reviser, with a reference or added entry under the original author.

The term 'new work' obviously points to the operation of the intellectual responsibility concept. The word 'substantially'
59

would again leave something to the subjective judgement of the cataloguer, and leave a certain area of debatable ground between existing works and new works. As it is stated, the rule can cope with many examples of revisions:

The Oxford Companion to English Literature
compiled and edited by Sir Paul Harvey.
Fourth Edition, revised by Dorothy Eagle.

In most cases the emphasis and wording of the title-page give adequate clues, although the rule itself obviously indicates that the heading will be determined by an examination of the work itself, and not merely its title-page. Because of this tendency to ignore the information as given on the title-page, AA (1908) ignores certain types of revision where the title-page information may be very important – where the name of the original author has become permanently identified with a work, and usually begins the title, even if, over the years, and through numerous editions, the work has been revised out of all recognition, as in the following example:

James Duff Brown's/ Manual/ of Library Economy/
Seventh Edition/ Completely rewritten/ by/ R.
Northwood Lock FLA/

The introduction reads: 'Not a page of the original remains, but the work was his, and his name will always be associated with it.'

The fields of law and medicine can provide numerous other examples of works revised over a long period of time to become virtually new works, but which are still identified by the name of the author of the original edition. The AA (1908) rule, as it stands, would obviously point to Lock as the main entry heading, but nothing could be worse than this. Entry must be under Brown, as the last part of the quotation indicates. In cases like this, a second principle must be brought into operation, that of the name most permanently associated with the work. AA (1908) introduces this principle in its rule for concordances, albeit wrongly, but fails to make use of it where it is needed, as an essential complement to the principle of intellectual responsibility.

The concept of intellectual responsibility is applied, correctly, to musical compositions (rule 8). The composer will receive main entry, and the author of the words in the case of
60

vocal music will receive an added entry. This rule is adequate for vocal music when the work concerned contains both the music and the words, but when we pass to a libretto (a separately published volume containing the words to which a piece of music has been set) we come up against a difficulty. AA (1908) in rule 9 regards such a libretto as an entirely independent work, and makes the theoretically correct decision to enter under the author of the words. It is more debatable whether this practically is the best entry. In cases where the libretto has little claim to significance on its own, its interest being entirely dependent on the music, a much more practical solution would be to enter under the composer, and regard the libretto as a dependent work. The words are subordinate to the music and both form a whole. The principle of the dependent work is invoked later in the case of supplements and indexes. The concept of the dependent work would be unsuitable for only one type of libretto — where the libretto has had a previous and independent existence of its own.

The principle of the dependent work is applied in AA (1908) in rule 15, for indexes to other publications, even when an index has its own author and title. The unity of the original work and its index is recognised; the index is dependent on the work which it indexes. Thus Palmer's index to the Times newspaper, though published separately and independently, would be entered under the 'Times'. An index to the works of a society or institution or other corporate body would be entered under the name of the body. There are, however, certain gaps in the rule for indexes. There is no provision for an index either to a single work of one author, or to his collected works. Rule 15 as it stands would seem to indicate that an index to the work of an author would be entered under his name, in the same way as an index to the publications of a corporate body, but it does not give any guidance to the *publications* of an author, unless this be regarded as a concordance, which is extremely unlikely. Presumably such an index would be entered under the name of its compiler, and entry under the author indexed would be regarded as subject entry. The reason for any distinction to be made between personal and corporate

61

authorship is hard to find. ALA (1949) would enter an index to a single work of a single author under the author of the original work, but an index to the *works* of a personal author would be entered under its compiler (rule 27).

Separately published indexes to a number of different publications have an existence and interest in their own right, and would be treated as separate publications, and entered under their own authors. Many such indexes are serial publications, for example the British Technology index, Library Literature, etc, and so would receive title entry.

In the case of choice between author and artist, rule 4 deals with what it terms 'Illustrators', a misleading term. One would hardly use the term 'Illustrator' for an artist, the reproductions of whose works make a complete volume, with little text. In later codes the term is widened to include any person whose creative works are represented pictorially - artist, photographer, sculptor, engraver, designer, etc. In all the codes the criterion of authorship is not really intellectual responsibility, but primary responsibility for the work in hand. Which is the major contribution, the work of the writer of the text, or that of the artist whose work is reproduced? This is so in AA (1908), entry being under the name of the person whose contribution forms the major part of the work:

> Enter books consisting solely of illustrations,
> or illustrated works of which the illustrations
> are the chief feature, under the illustrator or
> designer . . . If the illustrations are secondary
> in importance to the text, the book is to be entered
> under the name of the author, with added entry
> under the name of the illustrator.

The rule as it stands would appear to be adequate for those works consisting of reproductions of an artist's work, with the text as a subsidiary commentary, or with an introduction written by someone other than the artist, for example:

> Hogarth/ (1697-1746)/ with an introduction and
> notes/ by/ W. Gaunt/ Faber Gallery/

For this type of publication the rule gives obvious guidance. Conversely, when the work to be catalogued is an 'illustrated work', with the text as the principal element, the rule is also adequate:

62

> A Christmas carol/ a ghost story of Christmas/
> Charles Dickens/ with the original coloured
> illustrations by John Leech/

Just as obviously, the main entry must be under Dickens. In
doubtful cases, the author of the text is to be preferred. A
doubtful case would be where the writer of the text and the
artist (in many modern books the photographer) have
collaborated to produce a work where both elements are
important. The role played by each is not always clear from
the title-page, for example:

> W alter Kupper/ Pia Roshardt/ Cacti/ Translated and
> edited by Vera Higgins, M.A., V.M.H./ Nelson/ 1960/

From this title-page alone, and without previous knowledge of
the persons named on the title-page, one is not to know that
each was responsible for one facet of the book. There seems
a strong argument for entering under the name of the person
named first on the title-page, as is indicated in AACR (1967).
Emphasis throughout this section of the rules on the
'predominant' feature of a work indicates a tendency to ignore
the title-page, and catalogue according to hidden information
found only after an examination of the complete volume. In
the great majority of cases the emphasis and order of names on
the title-page is sufficient guidance.

A similar situation exists with commentaries (rule 13).
Again, choice is based on primary responsibility for the work,
but again, the title-page usually gives fairly reliable guidance
as to which element preponderates.

The other rules in this section of AA (1908) are based on the
intellectual responsibility concept. One rule does, however, give
rise to comment – rule 21 for translations, which correctly
enters translations under the heading for the original work. But,
this rule, taken in conjunction with rule 118, Anonymous –
Translations, where the two committees failed to agree, offers
an example of inconsistency on the part of the American
Committee. The Americans would enter translations of
anonymous works under their translated titles, a rule which
directly contradicts rule 21. The British were at least consistent,
and entered under the original title.

Corporate authorship

The problems of corporate authorship occupy a large section of
AA (1908). Many of the rules are concerned with the form of
name to be used for a corporate body in the heading, rather
than with the more fundamental problem of entry under the
name of a corporate body or some other element in the title.
This pre-occupation with the form of name of corporate body
overshadows the other problem, which is very poorly treated in
AA (1908). Since 1908 this has become a much more acute
problem with the expansion of the activities of corporate bodies
in various publishing directions. The problem of when to make
entry under a corporate body is partially treated in the
definition of corporate entry found in AA (1908):

Entry under names of bodies or organizations
for works published in their name or by their
authority.

The definition is far from adequate. The phrase 'published in
their name or by their authority' leaves many problems wide
open, and is not sufficiently definite as a practical working
guide. In its narrowest interpretation it would cover routine
administrative publications, for example:

BRITISH COUNCIL
    Annual report . . .

However, the real problem lies with those publications issued
under the imprint of a corporate body, but which also contain a
personal name on the title-page. Where the corporate body
merely acts as the publisher, it cannot claim main entry, as for
example with such publishing societies as the Early English Text
Society, the Chetham Society, etc. Yet the definition of
corporate entry quoted above would seem to cover such
instances. In other words 'in their name or by their authority'
would imply something more than a mere publishing activity
on the part of a corporate body. Apart from this, and the case
cited above, the definition does not help us very much in
deciding between a personal and a corporate name on a title-
page. On what should our criterion be based? The only
satisfactory criterion is that of intellectual responsibility for the
views, etc expressed in the publication. In such circumstances
AA (1908) gives little guidance. The guidance that is given is
misleading, and has been the source of much misinterpretation.

It is contained in rule 60, which reads as follows:
Reports not by an official. Enter under the writer
reports made to a department by a person who is
not an official, with added entry under the name
of the department.
A footnote to the rule reads: 'This rule may be applied also
in dealing with publications of private firms or companies,
the main entry usually being made under the name of the firm
when the compiler or editor is a regular official and the work
of compilation or editing is part of his official duties. On the
other hand, main entry is made under the individual when it is
known that the work is his own private publication. In either
case, added entry or reference is made under the party not
selected as the main heading.'

Apart from the fact that this rule would appear to
refer only to government publications and those of commercial
firms, ignoring societies and institutions, the choice of entry is
based on a completely irrelevant criterion so far as cataloguing
the publication is concerned — whether or not the personal
writer is an official of the corporate body. This is far removed
from the realities of the title-page and also from the concept of
intellectual responsibility. It has also given rise to such mis-
conceptions as the criterion of the 'paid official'.[1] In defence
of AA (1908) it could be said that the rule dealt specifically with
the reports to a department of government or private firm or
company, and was obviously not intended to cover all publications with both a personal and a corporate name on their title
pages. But the basis of the distinction is irrelevant to the
cataloguing problem. For example, Lionel McColvin was an
official of the Library Association when he published his
famous report in 1942. The report was published by the Library
Association, and bore its name as well as McColvin's, but to
enter it under the Library Association would be to violate the
concept of intellectual responsibility. It could be argued that
entry is under McColvin because he was an honorary and not a
paid official of the Association, but to do so would be to
catalogue the work by an economic criterion far removed from
the problems presented by the title-page. In the event, the
Library Association subsequently published its own proposals

1   Dorothy M Norris. Primer of cataloguing, London, 1952, pp 51-52

which did not entirely coincide with those expressed by McColvin.

ALA (1949) attempts to improve the situation, and does succeed in making matters a little clearer. In the second paragraph of rule 71 there is the following statement:

Monographic works by individual officials, officers, members and employees of corporate bodies, when these works are clearly not administrative or routine in character, are preferably to be entered under the personal author, even though issued by the corporate body.

This is more or less repeated in rule 75C (2). Rule 75C (1) would enter administrative reports made by an official as part of his routine duty under the department, and, conversely, in rule 75D reports made to a department by a writer who is not an official would be entered under the writer. Again the word 'official' keeps recurring, and again these statements are only made in the section on government publications. There is no comparable statement in the sections on societies and institutions. How difficult of interpretation these rules are may be gathered from the following examples quoted by Hal Draper from the catalogue of an American university library.[1]

1   U.S. Library of Congress
        Writings and addresses of Luther Harris
     Evans, librarian of Congress, 1945-1953.
     Washington, 1953.

2   MacLeish, Archibald
        The reorganization of the Library of
     Congress, 1939-1944 . . . (n.p. 1944)

3   The Case against the Saturday review of
        literature; the attack of the Sat. rev.
     on modern poets and critics, answered
     by the Fellows of American Letters of the
        Libr. of cong. . . . Chicago, Poetry, 1949.

The first example offends against rule 71, the second against

1 Hal Draper. How to roll back the corporate empire. *Library resources* 5 (1) Winter 1961, pp 73-81.

rule 75C (1). MacLeish was Librarian of Congress from 1939 until 1944, and this might have been published immediately after he retired although this seems doubtful. But such a comment illustrates how wrong it is to base the choice of heading on the criterion of being or not being an official of the corporate body concerned. The criterion is bibliographically irrelevant. The third example is even more curious. Here we have a corporate body adequately named on the title-page — Fellows of American Letters of the Library of Congress — and yet this has been ignored for the choice of heading in favour of the title. This is plainly cataloguing according to the Prussian Instructions.

Another area of considerable growth of publication since 1908 is that of the published reports of proceedings, symposia, etc. of conferences, congresses, and similar organizations. The conference usually has a name descriptive of its character, the published proceedings nearly always have also an editor named on the title-page, and at least one corporate body acting as a sponsor. A typical example would be the following:

Intrex/Report/ of a Planning Conference on/ Information Transfer Experiments, / September 3, 1965/ Edited by/ Carl F.J. Overhage and R. Joyce Harman/ Sponsored by/ The Independence Foundation/ of Philadelphia, Pennsylvania/ The M.I.T. Press/ Massachusetts Institute of Technology,/ Cambridge, Massachusetts, and London, England/ . . ./

With this type of publication the problem of personal versus corporate authorship is acute, and the only satisfactory criterion is again that of intellectual responsibility. AA (1908) deals with the problem in rule 105 (2):

Enter conventions and conferences of bodies
which have no existence beyond the convention
under the name of the convention. If no name
can be found, enter under the place of meeting
and supply a name descriptive of the character
of the meeting.

Apart from the fact that there is no mention of editorship or sponsorship by a corporate body, the rule, when the convention does not have a name, falls back on the usual procedure of AA (1908) and enters under place. The supplying of a name descriptive of the character of the meeting is of course bibliographically irrelevant, and to be effective depends on the ability of the cataloguer to choose that description which will also be chosen by the user of the catalogue, by no means a certain process.

Subordinate bodies and affiliated societies
Stemming from the distinction made in AA (1908) between societies and institutions, is the inconsistent treatment accorded to different types of subordinate organization. If the subordinate organization is institutional in character, it is not accepted as an author of its publications, even if its name is distinctive. According to rule 84, the Bodleian Library, being a university institution, must be entered under Oxford University, in spite of the fact that it has a particularly distinctive name. However, some other institutions, such as observatories, which are subordinate parts of a larger whole, may be entered under their own names, if they are situated at some distance from the parent body and have only a nominal connection with it. How far such a subordinate body must be separated from its parent body to qualify for individual entry is not stated, but the rule surely demonstrates one of the most bibliographically irrelevant conditions in any code of rules. On the other hand, affiliated or subordinate societies are recognised as authors by rule 79, if they have individual names which do not include the name of the parent organization:
    Scottish Library Association.
Similarly, subordinate departments of government may be entered directly under the name of the country or other jurisdiction without the intervention of any higher department in the heading if the name of the subordinate office is self-contained and distinctive and not common to a number of departments, and also (unsaid in AA (1908)) that they are not institutions in the meaning of the term used in AA (1908). Thus:
    GREAT BRITAIN.   *Office of scientific and technical information*
Rather than:
    GREAT BRITAIN.   *Department of education and science. Office of scientific and technical information*
The National Physical Laboratory at Teddington, however,
68

which is part of the Ministry of Technology, would be entered under Teddington and not under the Ministry because it is an institution according to the definition of an institution in AA (1908).

Government publications
There is usually less comment about the first category of corporate authorship in AA (1908) – Government publications. This is surprising because this section, more than most, introduces all sorts of bibliographically irrelevant concepts. In AA (1908) units of government, military, civil and ecclesiastical, are considered authors of their official publications (rule 58). The rule also attempts to delimit the concept of governmental authorship by stating that the names of departments, bureaus, etc from which the publications emanate are to be used as subheadings under the name of the country, etc. Clearly, then, government publications are limited to those of actual departments of government, and do not include those from other governmental bodies. The latter are not treated in AA (1908), and we are left to assume that they will be treated according to the other rules for corporate authorship, *ie* as societies or institutions as the case may be. The use of the name of the department as a subheading to the name of the governmental unit results in headings which practically never appear on title-pages. For example, a publication of the Ministry of Health will not have 'Great Britain' printed on the title-page, though the name of the department will be there. This obviously gives rise to difficulties on the part of the user of the catalogue. Does he know of the cataloguing convention to interpose the name of the country or other unit of government before the name of the department, and also of the use of Great Britain, rather than Britain? Even if the user of the catalogue knows of such conventions it is hardly likely that he will appreciate the further distinction between the entry of government publications under the name of the place or other area *as author,* and entry under place as a substitute for name entry for institutions. The distinction is maintained in AA (1908) by punctuation and underlining, though the situation becomes confused when institutions controlled by government are entered under place. The collection of government publications
69

under the name of the governmental unit is presumably dictated by the assumption that confusion might follow direct entry under the name of the department, if several countries or other governmental units have departments with identical names. The assumption has not been proved, and the rule results in vast accumulations of entries under names of countries. By 1950, the Library of Congress had 212 drawers of entries under 'United States'.[1] An alternative ruling for the smaller library in favour of direct entry under the name of the issuing department would be more in line with actual practice in most libraries. It would also coincide with the practice of most official bibliographies of government publications issued in this country and in the United States. The rule itself is in contradiction with rule 79 for Affiliated societies, which, as we have seen, are to be entered under their own names if self-sufficient for identification purposes.

The section on government publications also illustrates how inadequate AA (1908) is for present-day needs. The extension of government into so many spheres of public life has given rise to a great volume of government publications for which there is little guidance in the code. If rule 58 is interpreted strictly, the official publications of nationalised undertakings and institutions would not be entered under the name of the country, but under their own names:

National Coal Board
British Broadcasting Corporation
British Rail

But, if such an organization is the direct responsibility of a member of the cabinet, it would be entered under the name of the country:

GREAT BRITAIN.   *Post Office*

To find the correct heading for this type of corporate body, the user of the catalogue must be certain of the exact position occupied by the body concerned in the governmental administrative structure. This again illustrates the tendency of AA (1908) to base rules, not on the bibliographical problem involved by the title-page information, but on purely irrelevant criteria. To the user of the catalogue, the status of the Post Office and

1   Mortimer Taube. The cataloging of publications of corporate authors. *Library quarterly* 10 (1) January 1950, 1-20.

the British Broadcasting Corporation would probably appear to be similar. When the Post Office becomes a nationalised undertaking similar to the British Broadcasting Corporation in the near future and ceases to be directly controlled by a government department, the entries will then have to be altered. Given that there will then be more consistency in the catalogue between the headings for similar bodies, the present rule illustrates how wrong it is to base cataloguing rules on criteria which are bibliographically remote from the problems presented by the title-page.

When such bodies are to be entered under their own names, one must presume that they are to be treated as ordinary (non-government) corporate bodies, *ie* as societies or institutions as the case may be, and governed by the same rules of entry:

London.   Science museum

Teddington.   National physical laboratory

East Kilbride.   National engineering laboratory

The occurrence of the 'Victoria and Albert Museum, *South Kensington'* in this form as an example to rules 83 and 89B would confirm this view.

National institutions are covered by rule 90, where it is clearly stated that only those institutions which include the name of the country in their own names are to be regarded as national. Otherwise entry is made under the name of the place where the institution is located, unless the name begins with a proper noun or adjective, as is the case with the Victoria and Albert Museum, cited above. However, an examination of the Library of Congress Book Catalogue will reveal that three specific examples of the same type of institution would be entered differently. The British Museum would be entered under its name, according to rule 83. The Bibliotheque Nationale would be entered under Paris, according to rule 82, and the Library of Congress under United States according to no rule in the book. All are examples of the type of institution which might be regarded as 'national', yet none of them come within the operation of rule 90. It is perhaps ironic that these special rules and exceptions to general rules have been introduced into the code in deference to Cutter's 'convenience of the public' principle. They merely make our catalogues more involved and difficult to follow by the persons we are allegedly trying to help.

71

Another area where AA (1908) gives little guidance is that covering the reports of committees, commissions, etc, appointed by the government to report to it on matters of current concern. Such bodies have usually been treated as temporary departments of government, and have been entered under the name of the country, with their own names as sub-headings:

GREAT BRITAIN. *Royal commission on the press,*
It would seem to be more in line with the philosophy of AA (1908) to enter the publications of such bodies directly under their own names, even if this would mean cumulating entries under common words such as 'commission' 'committee', etc. On the criterion of intellectual responsibility, the country cannot be regarded as author, since the report of a committee represents only the committee's views and not those of the government which appointed it. Such committees are usually specifically appointed by a minister of the crown, but they cannot be catalogued under the name of the department for the same reason. Each has a chairman, but the same reasons would forbid entry under his name.

Similarly, laws are regarded as official publications of a country, city or other unit of government, and form a large and important body of government publications. The problem of their cataloguing lies not so much in the fact that they are government publications, but that they comprise a body of similar material issued under the name of the government unit promulgating them. To enter, however, the text of each law or statute under the name of the country and then the title would scatter similar material. For this reason AA (1908) uses a form subdivision — 'Statutes' after the name of the country. It should be noted however, that this is form entry rather than author entry, and is probably inevitable. It would however, be more consistent with the authorship principle of AA (1908) to enter laws under the name of the legislative body enacting them, than to give them form subheadings under the name of the country. Cutter preferred entry under the name of the legislative body.

AA (1908) understandably does not cater for government publications detailing the application of the law, *ie*, in this country, statutory instruments. There would seem to be a stronger case here for entry under a form subheading than for

72

laws, unless entry is made under the name of the ministry or department responsible for them .

Anonymous and pseudonymous works
In accordance with the literary unit concept, AA (1908) does not accept anonymous works at their face value without an attempt being made on the part of the cataloguer to determine authorship.
Rule 112 states:
> Enter anonymous works under the name of the
> author when known, otherwise under the first
> word of the title not an article. Make added
> entries for titles of all anonymous works
> whose authors are known; when the work relates
> to a particular person or place make added
> entry also under this name.

In every case an attempt should be made to ascribe authorship. The added entry under title is, of course, necessary to guide the user of the catalogue who knows the work only by its title as given on the title-page. The added entries under names of persons and places are obviously subject entries, and have no proper place in a code of author cataloguing rules. If the rule had read: 'Make added entry under the name of a person or place named in the title'. (which it does not) one could have seen a connection between this rule and the British Museum practice of title entry for anonymous works under a 'person or place named or adequately described in the title'. The rule as it stands does not suggest that these added entries under persons or places are in any sense catchword title entries.

The rule for anonymous works also suffers from the AA (1908) code's arrangement by solution rather than by problem, already referred to. It is separated from the rule for pseudonymous works (rule 38). Both rules cover different aspects of the same general problem, that of concealed or undiscovered authorship. If authorship is concealed, and undiscovered, entry is made under the pseudonym, provided it is an assumed name under which a person writes. If it is a mere description of the author, which is not acceptable as a pseudonym, the work is treated as anonymous. Nowhere does AA (1908) adequately define 'pseudonym' or distinguish pseudonymous works clearly from

73

anonymous works. The wide separation of the two rules makes a difficult problem even more difficult. Within the context of intellectual responsibility and literary unit the distinction is important. If an author consistently employs one pseudonym (undiscovered) the literary unit is still maintained because entry would still always be under the one pseudonym. But, if the author, instead of a pseudonym, uses a consistent description which cannot be regarded as a pseudonym, each work would be treated as anonymous and entered under title. Thus they would be scattered throughout the catalogue, and the literary unit destroyed. The fact that authors do not consistently use one pseudonym, and that a descriptive phrase may cloak a number of different writers does not really nullify the above argument because every undiscovered pseudonym may represent a break in the literary unit. The situation is further aggravated by the fact that AA (1908) does not recognise initials as pseudonyms (rule 115) but would enter works in which the author's name is represented by initials under the first word of their titles. This in itself must constitute a breach in the literary unit. Consistency to the principle of intellectual responsibility would dictate some modification of the rules for anonymous and pseudonymous works in AA (1908).

Anonymous works present a considerable problem to any code which emphasises the intellectual responsibility concept. All anonymous works whose authors remain undiscovered represent a gap in the intellectual responsibility coverage of the catalogue for some writers. The same does not hold for undiscovered pseudonyms, unless several pseudonyms are used by the one person. Pursuance of the literary unit does not dictate entry under any given name or form of name. Insistence on the real name of the author does not in itself mean that the literary unit will be maintained. As L Jolley states 'undiscovered pseudonyms are as numerous as undiscovered murders'.[1]

1   L Jolley. Principles of cataloguing, London, 1961, p 10.

6
ALA PRELIMINARY SECOND EDITION, 1941

Revision of AA (1908) had been actively pursued during the
nineteen thirties between committees on both sides of the
Atlantic. The outbreak of the second world war in 1939 stopped
any further consideration on the British side. The American
Library Association continued its work of revision, and
published its Preliminary Second Edition in 1941.[1] ALA (1941)
is a direct descendant of AA (1908); its basic philosophy is the
same, its coverage is similar, *ie* rules for headings for author/
title catalogues, and for the description of the items entered
under these headings. The only alteration was an increase in the
number of rules to cover more specific problems and types of
publication which had appeared since 1908. 'The preliminary
edition, published in 1941, expanded the rules of 1908 to make
more provision for special classes of material.'[2]

ALA (1941) received a mixed reception in the United States.
The proliferation of the rules for entry was regretfully accepted
by a part of the profession as inevitable, though strongly
criticised by others who did not concede the inevitability of
such proliferation. The second part, covering the rules for
description, was much less enthusiastically received. The code
as a whole prompted Andrew D Osborn to write his famous
'Crisis in cataloging' article.[3] The reaction to ALA (1941) was
summed up by Seymour Lubetzky when he stated that 'A
considerable section of the profession was earnestly perturbed

1   American Library Association. ALA catalog rules: author and title entries;
prelim 2nd ed, Chicago, 1941.
2   American Library Association. ALA cataloging rules for author and title entries;
2nd edition, Chicago, 1949. Pref, p viii.
3   Andrew D Osborn. *op cit*
75

when confronted with the trend [towards more and more rules] and thought that the time had come to re-evaluate the rules in the light of objectives and principles.'[1]

The result was renewed revision of the rules, this time jointly by the American Library Association and the Library of Congress. Congress started to revise its rules for descriptive cataloguing in 1943 with a view towards simplification and the omission of all non-essential descriptive matter. The culmination was the publication of the Library of Congress rules for descriptive cataloguing in 1949.[2] In 1944 the American Library Association instructed its Catalog Code Revision Committee to proceed with the revision of Part 1 of ALA (1941) in the light of contemporary criticism. Further work on Part 2 was deferred. Miss Clara Beetle, of the Library of Congress, was appointed editor in 1946, and three years later the American Second Edition was published.[3] This edition omitted all rules for description, these being supplied by the Library of Congress 'Rules for descriptive cataloging'.

1 Seymour Lubetzky. Development of cataloging rules. *Library trends, 1953, 179-186.*
2 U S Library of Congress. Rules for descriptive cataloging in the Library of Congress. Washington D C, 1949.
3 American Library Association. ALA cataloging rules for author and title entries; 2nd ed edited by Clara Beetle. Chicago, 1949.

7
AMERICAN LIBRARY ASSOCIATION SECOND EDITION, 1949

In spite of the statement by the chairman of the Code Revision Committee that revision should proceed in the light of contemporary criticism, ALA (1949) is basically constructed on the same formula as AA (1908) and ALA (1941), though there is some attempt in the introduction by the editor to set out the principles upon which the code is constructed. However much we may disagree with the principles stated, is some consolation to know that there were some basic principles, which were absent from both previous codes. The principles were stated as follows:

1 The code is intended to represent the best or most general current practice in cataloguing in the libraries of the United States. The then current practice in the United States was based essentially on Cutter's rules for main entry, and his idea that the catalogue user was the final arbiter of the form that any specific rule should take. Allied to Cutter's practice was the custom built up over forty years by hundreds of cataloguers in the Library of Congress displayed on the entries on the printed catalogue cards distributed throughout the United States.

2 'The finding-list function of the catalog is extended beyond what is required for the location of a single book to the location of literary units about which the seeker has less precise information'. Here the basic concept of the literary unit which had been implied throughout AA (1908) is expressly stated, deriving from Miss Pettee's historical analysis of the further development of Cutter's rules[1]

3 'Exceptions or qualifications are made when too strict

1   Julia Pettee. *op cit.*

an application of a general rule would result in a heading not giving the most direct approach'. Here we have the restatement ·of Cutter's 'Convenience of the public' concept at the cost of 'system and simplicity'. Cutter's concept has had rather a curious history. It did not appear as part of his rules, but was added to the last part of his preface to the 4th edition of 1904, largely as an afterthought. Even then, it was directed not so much to the makers of cataloguing rules, but rather towards cataloguers themselves in their interpretation and application of a code. The concept was tacitly acknowledged by the framers of AA (1908), but in ALA (1949) it is acknowledged as the authority for the exceptions and qualifications to general rules, which abound. Thus the third objective in ALA (1949) which assumes more importance than the others traces its origin to a chance addition to Cutter's rules, where it was obviously directed to cataloguers rather than to code-makers. This, and the preceding statement also illustrate the antithesis between the collocative and the direct catalogue; the problem of cataloguing the one work as a unique item and also as one of a number of similar items. Further on the editor states: 'Similar good judgement is needed in extending and adapting the general rules to problems not specifically covered'. It could, of course be remarked that if there are to be exceptions to the general rules their consistent application to particular problems is made difficult, if not impossible.

Again, it is the first section of the code which is of most interest to us — 1. Choice of Main Entry. The general rule for authorship is similar to that in AA (1908) :

Rule 1.   Enter a work under the name of its author, whether personal or corporate.

In a note to the rule, the editor restates the case for intellectual responsibility as the determinant of the heading:

The author is considered to be the person or corporate body chiefly responsible for the intellectual content of the book, literary, artistic or musical.

Rule 2 restates the same position, and is to a large extent redundant:

Enter a work under the name of its author when known, whether or not his name appears

78

on the publication. Enter revisions and
other modifications under the original
author whenever the work remains substantially
his, especially if the book purports to
be an edition of the original work.

The second phrase of the first sentence makes it quite clear
that the cataloguer is not confined to title-page information, or
even to information to be found in the work being catalogued, but
may have to use extra-bibliographical information. The second
sentence would appear to make the distinction between the
'author' as the original writer or conceiver of a work as opposed
to an editor or reviser. This would appear to be needless in view
of the note appended to rule 1.

Thus, for works of single authorship, ALA (1949) would
choose that person for entry who is judged to be intellectually
responsible for the work, whether or not this appears on the
work itself.

Multiple authorship

In the case of multiple authorship, as defined earlier in relation to
AA (1908), ALA (1949) improves on the situation, though the
whole topic is still not treated in a unitary fashion. Rules 3 to 5
bring together works of multiple authorship where each author
or contributor performs a similar function in relation to the work.
Rules 6 to 19 cover 'Works of special type', the special type
being largely, but not entirely, the physical form of the work –
manuscript, maps, music, radio scripts, works of art etc. Many
of the rulings in this section are already covered by rule 1 and
its accompanying note, and are thus redundant. Multiple
authorship comes back with rules 20 to 29 in 'Works related
to previous publications'. These cover material which we have
previously described as 'Differentiated multiple authorship' when
discussing AA (1908). They include revisions, abridgements,
parodies, indexes, concordances, etc. Corporate bodies as
authors, though covered by rule 1 are treated separately in
Section III, rules 71 to 149.

Undifferentiated multiple authorship

Three types of undifferentiated multiple authorship are
distinguished:

79

1 Joint authorship, where the contribution of each collaborator is not usually separable from that of the others. Unlike AA (1908) this does not now include correspondence.

2 Composite works, *ie* original works produced by the collaboration of two or more authors in which the contribution of each forms a separate and distinct part, although included within a planned whole.

3 Collections, *ie* three or more separate works or parts of works, not forming a treatise or monograph on a single subject, combined and issued together as a whole.

All three categories are treated differently. Joint authors are entered under the author first named on the title-page, with added entries under the others included in the transcript of the title-page. The added entries would have the designation *joint author* suffixed to the name in the heading. If the work is obviously the chief responsibility of one author, the making of added entries will depend on the nature of the work, the number of collaborators, and the importance of their contributions. Composite works are entered under the author chiefly responsible, with added entries under the others, without the designation *joint author*, when their contributions warrant the entry. Presumably the author chiefly responsible need not necessarily be the first mentioned on the title-page, though in many cases he would be. If no principal responsibility can be ascribed, and there are not more than three collaborators, entry is to be made under the one first mentioned on the title-page; if more than three, under title. Collections with a collective title are generally entered under the editor, but if the title is distinctive and the work of editing appears to be slight, entry will be made under the title, *ie* similarly to composite works by more than three authors without designation of principal responsibility.

So far from being based on the intellectual responsibility concept, this set of rules would appear to depend rather on the concept of the name most prominent on the title-page, and, in certain instances, on the concept of principal responsibility. Principal responsibility is a new concept not present in AA (1908). It may be difficult to determine, and may not necessarily be apparent from the title-page. Moreover, it is to some extent dependent on a subjective judgment on the part of the cataloguer, and is to that extent unwelcome. The whole situation is obviously confused for the user of the catalogue. To have direct access to a heading he must be aware of the existence of the three categories of multiple authorship, and also of the various sub-categories, the significance of the number three for composite works, and must make an assessment of the contribution of an editor in the case of a collection. This is asking the user of the catalogue to make intellectual distinctions which he would find hard to justify, always assuming that he is aware that the work he is looking for is an example of multiple authorship, and he does not know the work by the name of only one of its authors. Without this prior knowledge the catalogue must present a mass of inexplicable differing practices and inconsistent rulings to the unversed user. A measure of simplifications was obviously needed. It was supplied by the *Code of cataloging rules* (1960) in which composite works and works of joint authorship are amalgamated under the single heading of 'Works of shared authorship'.

Lubetzky, in his *Cataloging rules and principles* (1953) was particularly destructive in his criticism of this section of ALA (1949), pointing out that there were sixteen rules in all covering this condition of authorship. 'When we design a rule for a specific *case*, rather than the condition illustrated by it, we create the necessity for duplicating that rule for every new case which may be encountered under different circumstances[1]. Lubetzky also calls attention to the examples to rules 4 & 5, which would appear to exemplify rules other than those to which they are appended.

The section on multiple authorship in ALA (1949) is typical of the code as a whole — proliferation of rules to cover specific cases, and the almost complete absence of any principles of entry, in spite of the statement in the introduction. The result is that proliferation also results in inconsistencies.

Differentiated multiple authorship
Here again we have a multiplicity of rules spread out over two subsections of the code — Works of special type (rule 6 to 19), and Works related to previous works (rules 20 to 29). Between them, the rules in this section cover all those cases of multiple

1   Seymour Lubetzky. Cataloging rules and principles, Washington, 1953.

81

authorship where the authors named on the title-page have exercised different functions, revising, editing, adapting, or translating, etc the work of another author (Works related to previous works). The first section (Works of special type) appears to be a miscellaneous group of rules applying to certain types of publication exhibiting certain specialised forms of authorship, *eg* heraldic visitations, musical compositions, manuscripts, etc. They extend the concept of authorship to other forms of printed and manuscript material — radio scripts, mediumistic writings, atlases, etc. In so doing the criterion of intellectual responsibility is again the principal determinant of authorship. In some cases this eagerness to ascribe authorship is carried to unhelpful limits. Rule II, for example, directs that mediumistic writings are to be entered under the medium rather than the supposed spirit whose alleged messages he transmits, in spite of the fact that the spirit is nearly always given greater prom-inence on the title-page. Is this rule consistent with that for 'Ghost writings' (rule 3E) which are entered under the name of the original talker? Is the catalogue-using public going to appreciate the distinction between the two types of authorship?

Rules 6 to 19 intrude between undifferentiated and different-iated multiple authorship, and would possibly have been better removed to another section, as has now been done in AACR(1967) The principles are the same, but the number of cases has been greatly increased as compared with AA (1908). Many of the rules in this section could have been omitted, given an intelligent interpretation of rule 1, the basic rule. There is a marked tendency to include in this section rules for certail classes of publication just because the material takes a form other than that of the printed book. Is there any need, for example, in a section of the code dealing with the determination of the heading, for separate rules for maps and architectural drawings (rules 10 & 19F) if the basic principle of intellectual responsi-bility has been applied correctly and consistently, as it has in these two cases? The only types of material which merit special treatment in this section of the code are those which may demand entry under a heading other than that of the name of person to whom intellectual responsibility may be ascribed. For example, manuscripts known by a number in a collection (rule 9A5), ships logs (rule 160) under the name of the ship, and
82

not that of its commanding officer; film scenarios under the title of the film because films are always known by their titles (rule 15). These special materials are included not because they are manuscripts, maps or film scenarios, but, largely through convention, they have tended to become known by some name other than that of their 'authors'.

Works related to previous works
This section, covered by rules 20 to 29, is largely a re-statement and expansion of a similar section in AA (1908). The same principles apply, and the same inconsistencies are repeated. The rule for revisions does not cater for a revised edition of a work identified by the name of its original author. Rule 21, for translations, still does not include translations of anonymous works (rule 32G). The latter are still inconsistently entered under their translated titles.

Anonymous and pseudonymous works
ALA (1949) improves considerably on the arrangement already seen in AA (1908), with its unhelpful separation of the rules for anonymous and pseudonymous works. In the later code these are brought together under the heading 'Works of Doubtful or Unknown Authorship'. The heading itself is however incomplete, since it does not cover the first rule within the section, rule 30 for Pseudonymous works. A more comprehensive heading would have been 'Works of Doubtful, Unknown, or Disguised Authorship'. ALA (1949) also improves on its predecessor in its attempt to distinguish between anonymous and pseudonymous works. Rule 30 specifies a pseudonymous work as 'one by an author who writes under a false name'. The word 'name' is important. A name need not describe the person or thing to which it is attached or applied. The specification is extended to include: 1 Assumption of the name of another real person (Horacio Flacco); 2 Re-arrangement of the letters of a name (Olphar Hamst for Ralph Thomas); 3 Inverted spelling (Eidrah Trebor); 4 Use of forename or forenames only (Anthony Berkeley for Anthony Berkeley Cox); 5 Re-arrangement of the order of sur-name and Christian names; 6 Use as a surname of a specific word or phrase with or without a definite article (Sigma, Acutus, etc). The emphasis is obviously on the acceptance of a name which is

83

a unique label as a pseudonym, and the rejection of a description.

We have already dwelt at some length on the importance of pseudonymous works in relation to the concept of the literary unit when dealing with AA (1908), and repetition here is unnecessary. Like AA (1908) the real name of the author is always given preference for entry when it is known (rule 30A) but with some exceptions in favour of the pseudonym, exceptions which were not permitted in the previous code. Entry may be made under the pseudonym when:

1 The real name of the author is unknown, or the author wishes it withheld. This is perhaps the most pointless rule to appear in any code. What else can the cataloguer do, if the real name is unknown, and the pseudonym has been recognised as such, and falls within the definition of one of the categories listed above? The second part of the rule is even more pointless than the first. Presumably the whole point of an author's use of a pseudonym is to withold his identity.   The cataloguer must assume that this was the reason for the adoption of a pseudonym. It might also be argued that the second part of the rule allows entry under a pseudonym in all cases where a pseudonym has been recognised as such.

2 When the pseudonym has been fixed in literary history and biography, and is the name looked for by an informed reader. This seems very reasonable, and corresponds to Library of Congress practice. Reference might have been made to the use of dictionaries and histories of literature and biography in difficult cases. That there are difficult cases is made evident by the inclusion under the main rule of the example of entry under Clemens rather than Mark Twain. This exception is extended to include current popular authors who are known by a pseudonym rather than by a real name. The choice is between real name and one pseudonym. A current popular author using more than one pseudonym is not included in the extension of the rule.

3 When two or more writers have combined to write under one pseudonym, for example Sergeanne Golon.

Although in ALA (1949) there is some relaxation in favour of the pseudonym, the emphasis is still on the literary unit. Nowhere in this rule is there any indication that an author may be represented in the catalogue by more than one name. As stated earlier, acceptance of the literary unit does not necessarily entail the use of the real names of authors. The literary unit may be constructed round any name.

Anonymous works

According to ALA (1949) an anonymous work is one in which the author's name does not appear anywhere in the book. This is complete anonymity, but anonymity may also take the form of using a descriptive word or phrase in place of one's name. To the cataloguer the line of demarcation between anonymous and pseudonymous works becomes important. Rule 30 attempted to define pseudonymous works fairly closely. Likewise rule 32 extends the definition of anonymous works to the following situations:

1 Works in which the authorship only appears in a concealed manner, so that it is not obvious. In cases of doubt the work is to be treated as anonymous. There is a vagueness about this rule which is disconcerting. Does it mean that the author's name is hidden at the end of the work, or in the preface, or concealed by secret ink?

2 Works whose authorship is indicated by a descriptive or generic word or phrase, preceded by an article – 'A School-teacher', 'A Practising Librarian', etc. These substitutes for the author's name are descriptive and generic, and are thus not acceptable as pseudonyms.

3 Works, in which in place of his name, the author quotes the title of another work he has written.

4 Works in which the author uses initials, asterisks, or other symbols in place of his name. The exclusion of these substitutes for names from the pseudonymous category seems surprising, as they are unique, and in no way either descriptive or generic. Both the British Museum and Cutter would regard these as pseudonyms.

Works in which the author uses as a *name* a specific word or phrase with or without a definite article are treated as pseudonymous.

Again, as in AA (1908) the main rule for anonymous works is to enter them under their author when known, with added entry under their title, and added entry or reference for any phrase used in place of the author's name. The added entry under the

85

name of a person or place referred to in the work, as advocated by AA (1908) is dropped. The importance of the distinction between the two types of authorship has already been discussed in relation to AA (1908), and as the rules for the two types are substantively the same further discussion here would be repetitive.

Spurious works and works of doubtful authorship
This is a new category covered by rule 31, which states, in effect that works of ancient, classical or medieval writers which have been transmitted as theirs in manuscript, and have appeared in printed editions under their names, but have been later excluded from the canon of their genuine works, are still to be entered under these authors, with the subheading 'Spurious and doubtful works', provided the real authorship remains unknown or uncertain. With modern authors, if the authenticity of authorship has been disproved, main entry is made under the title.

Corporate authorship
The rules for corporate authorship in ALA (1949) follow the same pattern and are based on similar principles to those of AA (1908). In both codes the majority of the rules in this section are concerned with the manner in which these bodies should be entered. The same four groups of corporate bodies are recognised — governments, societies, institutions, and miscellaneous bodies. Because of the tremendous increase in government publishing between 1908 and 1949, and the prolifer-ation of all kinds of corporate bodies as authors, this has become the largest section in the code (79 rules). The form of name to be adopted for corporate bodies is not, however, our immediate concern. ALA (1949)'s treatment of the problems with which we are concerned in this paper — the acceptance of corporate bodies as authors, and the choice between corporate and personal entry — have already been introduced when discussing AA (1908) and need not be repeated here, except, perhaps, to repeat the ALA (1949) does give some more useful guidance on the problem of corporate versus personal entry than AA (1908), especially in rules 71 and 75C-D.

Very briefly, the nature of ALA (1949) has been summed up by one commentator as 'a diet rich in rules and poor in principles '.[1]

1 Source not known

8
CATALOGING RULES & PRINCIPLES, 1953

ALA (1949) did not please the profession. The proliferation of
rules was received with dismay by cataloguers and administrators,
but generally with less dismay by reference librarians in the
United States, who had become accustomed to a catalogue
which was rather more than a finding list. Cataloguers, in
particular, felt that there were certain areas in ALA (1949)
which required some research and re-thinking, particularly
within the field of corporate authorship. Seymour Lubetzky,
Bibliographic Consultant to the Library of Congress, who had
already made a study of the rules for descriptive cataloguing
which was embodied in the report by Herman H Henkle:
Studies of descriptive cataloging (1946) was asked by the
Board of Cataloging Policy and Research of the Division of
Cataloging and Classification of the American Library
Association to make a detailed analysis of ALA (1949), especially the rules for corporate authorship. The result of his
analysis was published in its third draft as *Cataloging rules
and principles: a critique of the ALA rules for entry and a
proposed design for their revision* (1953).

The main outline of this publication is so well known to
the profession that no detailed description of its contents will
be given here. Suffice to say that the Lubetzky report is in
four parts: 1 A critical examination of ALA (1949) with a
view to pointing out the unnecessary proliferation of rules,
and the resulting inconsistencies arising from the attempt
to make rules for specific types of publication without
consideration of the general principles underlying the specific
rules. 2 A similar analysis of the rules for corporate authorship,
working from the historical viewpoint and tracing the evolution
88

of the concept of corporate authorship in the United States from Cutter to ALA (1949), particularly JCM Hanson's distinction between societies and institutions which had so complicated the rules for corporate authorship in both AA (1908) and ALA (1949). 3 Design for a code, in which Lubetzky lays down the principles upon which any new code of rules should be based. 4 Answers to general questions raised as a result of the previous drafts.

Throughout his report Lubetzky is at pains to emphasise that the purpose of his report was not to effect a revision of the rules, but to clear the ground for agreement on the basic objectives which should underlie any new code. In his third section Lubetzky comes back to the age-old problem of the objectives of the author/title catalogue, and comes up with what is largely a restatement of those propounded by Cutter in 1876:

1 To enable the user of the catalogue to determine readily whether or not the library has the book he wants *ie* the finding-list function of the catalogue .

2 To reveal to the user of the catalogue, under one form of the author's name, what works the library has by a given author and what editions and translations of a given work *ie* the collocative catalogue .

These two objectives are only in conflict when an author uses different names on the title-pages of his books, or different titles are used for different editions and versions of his works. The problem then arises as to which objective should have priority. After some consideration, and a look at what Panizzi and James Duff Brown had to say, Lubetzky adopts an ambivalent attitude, and does not finally indicate the priority which should be accorded to the one objective or the other. The significance of this ambivalent attitude will be discussed later. Lubetzky would appear to favour the first objective when in conflict with the second, pointing out that ALA (1949) and AA (1908) occasionally sacrifice the first objective for the second. Both ALA (1949) and AA (1908) generally prefer either the earlier or full legal forms of name, or both, when a conflict arises, but Lubetzky points out that the second objective does not necessarily imply this. The first objective requires entry under the form of name by which an author is cited and identified. To enter all the works of an author under one form of name may involve changing entries
89

in the catalogue, whereas entry under *each* form as used will assure the permanence of the entries. But permanence of entry is not necessarily one of the prerequisites of an efficient catalogue. The British Museum rules, while assuring the permanence of the entries for individual books, in some cases separated them from other books by the same author or even other entries for the same work. After all, the use of names as found on title-pages is a relative matter. The line must be drawn somewhere; usually it is drawn at the different *names* used by an author, it is not extended to different *forms of name* used by the same author, even in these codes, such as Panizzi's, where the second objective is accorded much less importance. Even the British Museum rules, with their insistence on title-page forms, do not enter an author under more than one form of his name, though it will enter an author under the different names he has used, provided the different names take a form which the British Museum accepts as pseudonym.

Lubetzky, in his report, does seem partly to be returning to the British Museum policy of the authority of the title-page in choosing the form of name under which the literary unit should be collected. This is a considerable corrective to the previous codes' preference for the earliest form, *eg* AA (1908) (British edition) and the legalistic form, *eg* ALA (1949). Lubetzky develops his emphasis on the title-page information rather than on outside sources in his section on 'Bibliographic Conditions and Principles'. We have already criticised both AA (1908) and ALA (1949) for some of their rules based on bibliographically irrelevant criteria, for example corporate versus personal entry, and for the intellectual responsibility concept operating to produce headings which bear no relation to the information found on a particular title-page. 'The most important characteristic of a book for the purposes of cataloging is that it is provided with a prominent identification tag in the form of a title-page .... The title-page generally includes the name of the author and the title of the book, sometimes only the title of the book and occasionally only the name of the author. The name of the author and the title of the book are therefore the most important clues by which the book will be identified when cited, and by which it will be looked for in the catalog or called for in the library'.[1] In other words, a work will be identified by a particular title and author and in difficult cases the title-page itself will be the arbiter of which author and title will be chosen. This attitude is completely at variance with the intellectual responsibility concept pursued by the codes of 1908 and 1949.

In spite of the title of his report, to Lubetzky there are no principles of authorship as such. He states that his report 'deliberately omits mention of "principle of authorship". . . it concerns itself with the objectives of cataloging and the methods by which these objectives can be achieved'. To this extent the title of his report is misleading. To Lubetzky cataloguing principles are merely directives whereby the objects of a catalogue can best be achieved. 'The entry of a work under its author, or, in the absence of the author, under its title is a fundamental way of meeting the objectives of the catalog. However, it is not always obvious who should be regarded as the author when more than one individual is involved.., or which should be regarded as the title of the work when it has been issued under more than one title or under varying titles. Hence the need for directives to indicate how such conditions should be treated. There is, thus, no need for the recognition of any 'principle of authorship' any more than there is for any 'principle of titleship'[2].

Thus does Lubetzky dismiss the intellectual basis of authorship upon which the two previous codes had been constructed. This is consonant with his preference for the first objective when the two are in conflict. The concept of intellectual responsibility pursued by the codes of 1908 and 1949 will inevitably lead to a preference for the second rather than the first objective. As we have seen previously, the concept of intellectual responsibility may be inadequate to determine authorship in all cases where a choice of authors occurs. This is not to deny the validity of the concept; it is only to state that in itself it is insufficient, and can lead to a very indirect catalogue. Lubetzky's practice of regarding the title-page as the arbiter of author and title is also insufficient as a sole guiding principle or directive, as his section on 'Variant conditions and principles' attests. With his emphasis on the title-page, however, Lubetzky

1   Seymour Lubetzky. *op cit* pp 42-43
2   Seymour Lubetzky. *op cit* p 60

91

brings cataloguers back to bibliographical reality and to the practical commonsense of Panizzi more than one hundred years earlier. Panizzi did not attempt to define authorship, nor does Lubetzky.

Though Lubetzky was the first to emphasise that his *Cataloging rules and principles* was in no manner to be regarded as a code of rules, it received general approval, and in 1956 he was invited by the American Library Association to edit a new revision of ALA (1949). The result appeared in 1960 as: *Code of cataloging rules, author and title entry: an unfinished draft . . . 1960,* hereafter referred to as CCR (1960). This gave Lubetzky the opportunity to put into practice the measures he had recommended in his report, and was to form the basis of renewed co-operation between the American Library Association and the Library Association. CCR (1960) also formed the framework for the general agreement on cataloguing principles achieved internationally at Paris in 1961.

9
CODE OF CATALOGING RULES, 1960

CCR (1960) was prepared by Seymour Lubetzky for the Catalog Code Revision Committee of the American Library Association, and in it the objectives listed by Lubetzky in 1953 were repeated:

> The objectives which the catalog has to serve are two.
> 1 To facilitate the location of a particular publication, i.e. a particular edition of a work which is in the library.
> 2 To relate and display together the editions which the library has of a given work and the works which it has of a given author.
> The two functions are complementary, but both are essential to the effectiveness of the catalog.

These two functions of the author catalogue are very similar to those stated by Cutter in 1876 (see p 38). The main difference is in the use of the words 'work' and 'edition' in the later code in place of Cutter's use of the word 'book'. The latter blurs the distinction between 'work' and 'edition', and, as a result, in Cutter, AA (1908) and ALA (1949) the main entry sometimes represents 'work' and sometimes 'edition'. For example, in the rules for translations in both AA (1908) and ALA (1949) no guidance is given as to which title, original or translated, is to be used. The assumption is that each title is to be treated independently. In these rules the 'book' or 'edition' is the unit, whereas the 'work' is the unit in other rules — Anonymous classics, revisions, etc. This represents a lack of consistency in the construction of the main entry.

CCR (1960) makes quite clear that the function of the main entry is to identify the editions of a certain work by a certain

93

author under a particular title and a particular name. The 'work' not the 'edition' is the unit. Added entries and references are to be used to 'facilitate the location of the editions issued under other titles, and the works issued under the other names of the author'. The assumption is that the catalogue-user is interested in the work represented by the particular publication rather than in its embodiment in any particular edition. The alternative of treating each edition of a work as a distinct bibliographical entity, with added entries and references to link together the various editions of a work appearing under different titles, and the other works of an author appearing under different names is rejected. Thus, the two objectives, which may appear to be incompatible in certain circumstances are reconciled consistently and systematically for the first time by the method of entering each work under 'a particular title and a particular name'.

In so doing CCR (1960) avoids the use of the term 'Main entry' in the sense of the most important entry. It merely states that 'entry is made'. This recognises the fact that in multiple-entry catalogues using unit cataloguing methods the distinction between main and added entries is largely academic. However, in single entry catalogues, such as union catalogues, the distinction is important. But, as the primary function of union catalogues is the identification and location of specific bibliographical terms, *ie* 'editions', there would appear to be some advantage in using the alternative rejected by CCR (1960).

In its rules for determining authorship CCR (1960) is much broader in approach than ALA (1949). The former attempts to provide a comprehensive set of rules for all types of material, and at the same time including many different types of author-ship within the one rule, which were spread over many rules in ALA (1949).

The general rule for authorship is rule 1 :

a.   The work of a person, whatever the character
or the medium by which it is presented, is entered
under the name of the person as author of the
work presented.

(Note: The author is the person whose work is presented
or exhibited, not the one who prepared a particular
edition or presentation of the work. When the art or
skill of the performer is exhibited, the performer is

94

treated as the author of the work exhibited).
b. If the author is not named in the work but has
been established from other sources, his name is
supplied in brackets.

This is an obvious attempt to cover all types of material as well as printed books in one broad general rule. The utility of attempting to gather all types of material under one general rule of authorship may be questioned. For example, art librarians have always objected to the entry of reproductions of the works of artists under the artist rather than the introducer or commentator, regarding the entry under artist as subject entry. Certain types of material may not be amenable to or require author entry as such, and one has the impression that CCR (1960) occasionally forces author entry, presumably for the sake of consistency. It would enter an album of photographs of an actor in his various roles under his name. This would appear to be pushing the authorship concept rather too far, but is almost inevitable within the general framework of the philosophy of CCR (1960). In the examples cited above, subject entry under the artist and actor would be more appropriate. One commentator has pointed out that if the primary purpose of CCR (1960) is to record a work in such a way that the entry will be readily located in the catalogue, some other form of entry than the author's name may be more appropriate.[1] She cites the examples of Burke's Peerage and the Oxford Books of verse, which are generally better known by their titles than by any author element. CCR (1960) runs into difficulties later with its rules for treaties and constitutions (rule 42). Because of the 'particular title and named author' principle it is forced to reject the form entries given to these types of publication by the two previous codes, and as straight title entry would be unsatisfactory, it adopts a standard form of title. This is a change of form rather than of substance in the rules.

Another basic shaft of principle is seen in rule 2: Works of avowed authorship:
a. A work prepared by one person for another person in whose name it is presented is entered under the

1   Susan M Haskins. Stepping stone to a new catalog code. *Journal of cataloging and classification* 9 (3) September 1953, 127.

95

person who is purportedly responsible for it, with
an added entry under the person who prepared it.

The phrase 'purportedly responsible' makes the form in which
the information is presented on the title-page the sole arbiter
of authorship. This is in line with the importance attached by
Lubetzky to the title-page information, and represents a major
shift from the intellectual responsibility basis of authorship of
the previous codes. It is also consonant with the first objective
as stated at the beginning of the code, and helps to avoid any
tendency to construct catalogue entries according to hidden
and bibliographically irrelevant information only known to,
because discovered by the cataloguer, and facilitates direct
location of a work in the catalogue. Reliance on the title-
page information also lightens the cataloguer's task considerably. Determination of intellectual responsibility could be
a lengthy and involved task. This new approach may also help
to bridge the gap between library cataloguing practices and
those of publishers in their trade bibliographies and catalogues.

Multiple authorship
In its rules for multiple authorship CCR (1960) clears away all
the deadwood of redundant and repetitive rules for specific cases
of ALA (1949). Rule 3 covers Joint authorship, and, in effect,
combines rules 3 and 4 of ALA (1949). The CCR rule reads as
follows:
> A work produced by the collaboration of two
> or more persons, or representing an exchange
> (conversation, correspondence, debate,
> interview, symposium, etc.) between two or
> more persons is entered as follows:
> a. If one is represented as principal author,
> entry is under him. . .
> b. If no one is represented as principal author,
> and there are not more than three, entry is under
> the first author mentioned on the title-page.
> If more than three, entry is made under an
> editor, if named on the title-page, otherwise
> under title. A report by a person of an
> exchange with another person or persons is
> entered under the reporter, except when represented

as chiefly the work of another person.

This comprehensive rule disposes of many of the useless distinctions in ALA (1949). More particularly, it avoids the distinction between joint and composite authorship, a distinction which we have already criticised, and which is not generally supported by title-page evidence. Thus the rules are brought back to the title-page in the phrase 'represented as ... author' as opposed to ALA (1949)'s phrase 'under the author chiefly responsible' in relation to composite works (rule 4). The latter phrase does not infer any relation to the information set out on the title-page, but rather suggests that 'chief responsibility' is to be ascertained by the cataloguer from an examination of the complete work.

CCR (1960) still makes separate provision for anthologies and collections in rule 4, which corresponds to ALA (1949) rule 5:

> An anthology or collection, other than a
> series, compiled from the works of various
> authors, is entered under the compiler
> or editor, if named on the title-page, or
> under the title, with added entries under
> the author or authors and titles presented,
> as may be desirable.

This represents a clear-cut rule which is much simpler to apply than ALA (1949) rule 5. The subjective judgements required of the cataloguer by the earlier code are avoided. More importantly, the user of the catalogue no longer needs to appreciate the distinctions between the three types of multiple authorship of the previous code. The shift of emphasis is again towards the information presented by the title-page.

CCR (1960) introduces a new concept which is partly implied but not specifically stated in ALA (1949) — Works of changing authorship (rule 5):

> A work issued in successive editions which
> may be prepared by different compilers or
> editors, or one of a type which is normally
> so issued — directories, encyclopaedias, guide-
> books . . . or other standard reference work, is
> entered under its title.
> b. If the original compiler's name is included

in the title of the later editions, the entry
is under his name.

The phrase 'standard reference work' has been commented on by
one writer [1]. How can the cataloguer define a 'standard reference
work'? Can a new reference work be predicted to become a
'standard reference work' on first cataloguing it? This concept
is implicit, but not actually stated, in the ALA (1949) rule for
directories (rule 5E). Thus the Kroeger/Mudge/Winchell series
of editions of 'Reference books' would now have title entry.

This rule is necessary if the second objective is to be
fulfilled — entering all editions of the same 'work' under the
one heading in the catalogue, and though it may be consistent
and theoretically sound, it must inevitably result in some
confusion to the user of the catalogue. This user, not knowing
the publishing history of Kroeger, Mudge, and Winchell, and
knowing Winchell as the author of the seventh edition could
reasonably be puzzled by the title entry. The crux of the
matter would seem to lie in the definition of a 'work'. Can
Winchell's 'book' really be regarded as the 'work' of her two
predecessors? The title-page states that it is *based on* the work
of Mudge, which bears a slightly different title. This example
might have been better treated under rule 11 — Continuations,
supplements, related works:

11a. A work of a person which continues, supplements,
or otherwise relates to a work of another person, but is
published separately, is entered under its own author, with
added entry under the author and title of the other work.

Lubetzky obviously considered the above as 'editions' of the
same 'work', and ruled accordingly.

Differentiated multiple authorship
We have already distinguished this category of material in the
earlier codes. It is succinctly dealt with in six rules in CCR (1960)
under the title : *Editions, Translations, Revisions, and Related
works* (rules 7-12). Some of the rules in this section fill gaps
which existed in ALA (1949), for example, the rule for Editions
(rule 7) covers a situation for which no specific provision was
made in the previous code, *ie* editions in which little or no

1   Margaret Beckman. Experiment in the use of the revised code of cataloguing
rules. *Library resources* 5 (3) Summer 1961, 216-220.

revision took place. ALA (1949) covers editions in which
revision took place in rule 20, and rule 2 in the same code
states that revisions and other modifications are to be entered
under the original author whenever the work remains substantially his, especially if the book purports to be an edition
of the original work. This rule, and others, in this section of
CCR (1960) continue the emphasis on the 'work' rather than
the 'book'. Rule 7 introduces the concept of the 'uniform
title' for editions of a work appearing under different titles,
either subsequently or consecutively (rules 7b and 7c). 7d caters
for works with variant titles in different editions, but which have
a common phrase or significant word, for example:

Shakespeare's tragedy of *Hamlet*
The tragedy of *Hamlet*
Shakespeare's *Hamlet*
Hamlet, prince of Denmark.

The significant word in the title is underlined, and the entry
would be filed by it. Neither of the previous codes catered to
any great extent for uniform entry of variant titles. ALA (1949)
did so in the case of music. The entry of variant titles under
a uniform heading is necessary if the unit of cataloguing is to
be the 'work' rather than the 'book'. By rule 8 of CCR (1960)
translations are to be entered under their original titles,
with an exception in favour of translated titles for small popular
libraries which are likely to have the work only in translation.
Again, the emphasis is on the bibliographic unit.

The rule for revisions (rule 9) again emphasises the
importance of the title-page in deciding between the original
author and the reviser. Rule 9a reads:

A work which has been revised or brought up to date
but is issued under the name of the original author
is entered under the name of that author, with an
added entry under the reviser.

And 9b reads:

However, a revision issued under the name of the reviser
is entered under the reviser, with an added entry
under the author and title of the original work.

The words 'issued under the name of the original author/
reviser' mark a significant change from ALA (1949) with its
phrases such as 'substantially a new work' and 'substantially

99

that of the original author'. The latter obviously call for subjective judgements on the part of the cataloguer, which may be time-consuming to make, and which in the final analysis may be based on information not found on the title-page of the work concerned. The CCR (1960) rule also caters for the type of revision which we have already encountered — where the work is substantially a new work, but the original author's name is still closely identified with it, *eg* Brown's Manual or Gray's Anatomy.

Rule 10, for *Adaptations,* is both wider and more specific than ALA (1949), and again avoids asking the cataloguer to make a subjective judgement. Rule 11, *Continuations, supplements, and Related works* (already quoted) brings together a number of separate rules in ALA (1949) because it deals primarily with the conditions of authorship and publication, rather than with types of work. The criterion of authorship and publication is again emphasised on rule 12, for concordances and indexes, which are to be entered under their own authors as independent works, unless published with the original to which they refer.

Throughout this section, the emphasis is on authorship as indicated by the title-page of the work being catalogued (*cf* the definition of authorship as given in the note to rule 1) and not on the criterion of intellectual responsibility as employed in both AA (1908) and ALA (1949). Because of their preoccupation with the intellectual responsibility for the work concerned, both previous codes tended to ignore the information as given on the title-page, and base the heading on intellectual and subjective judgements of the cataloguer, which could bear little relation to the title-page and result in entries under obscure headings, as well as being time-consuming for the cataloguer. In CCR (1960) Lubetzky gives back to the title-page some of its earlier importance. CCR (1960) emphasises the first objective of the catalogue, ignored by the two previous codes in favour of the second. CCR (1960) by its complementary emphasis on the 'work' also goes far to achieve the second objective — to display together the editions which the library has of a given work and the works which it has of a given author. The two previous codes implicitly attempted to make the main entry satisfy the second objective, and the added entries the first, thus emphasising the second objective at the expense of the first.

CCR (1960) recognises the artificiality of the distinction between main and added entries, especially where unit cataloging is used, while at the same time making *entry* according to the conditions indicated by the title-page, thus emphasising the first objective, the location of a particular *publication*. But, because of its equal emphasis on the second objective, regarding a publication as 'one of the editions of a certain work by a certain author, to be identified under a particular title and a particular name' avoids the drawback of following the first objective alone, the separation of different editions of the same 'work'.

Corporate authorship
Perhaps one of the most distinctive features of CCR (1960) is its treatment of names of corporate bodies, particularly the abandonment of the distinction between societies and institutions which had bedevilled both AA (1908) and ALA (1949). As a result, all corporate bodies are to be entered under their names. The problem of the treatment of the names of corporate bodies is again outwith the scope of the present paper. One point is worth emphasising, however, and that is the clear distinction made in CCR (1960) between rules determining what shall be the heading for publications containing the names of corporate bodies on their title-pages, and rules for the name or form of name to be chosen for such bodies, once entry has been decided. This arises partly from the abandonment of any distinction between types of corporate bodies which we have referred to above. One other result of a uniform entry under name of corporate body is that the scope of corporate authorship is extended, and not limited as it was in the previous codes to those classified as societies, and institutions whose names begin with a proper noun or adjective (the others being entered under place rather than name).

As far as possible CCR (1960) attempts to bring corporate authorship within the framework of personal authorship, but with certain qualifications. This is stated in rule 21. In the following rules CCR (1960) makes much clearer the distinction between personal and corporate authorship. Rule 22 indicates fairly clearly the types of publication which are to be entered under the name of the corporate body: ·

101

A work which explicitly or implicitly represents
an act, communication, or product of the
activity of a corporate body is entered under the
name of that body . . . This includes (a) the
proceedings, transactions, debates, reports,
and other works produced by or issued in the name
of the corporate body; (b) administrative
regulatory and other official documents, such
as constitutions, rules, decisions, periodic
reports of activities, announcements, guides,
catalogs — which, even if prepared by an
individual, implicitly bear the authority of
the corporate body; and (c) works issued by
a corporate body, other than a commercial
publisher, without the name of an author or
compiler, and not represented as anonymous
works.

The above represents a much fuller and precise definition of
those instances where a corporate body can be considered as
author of publications issued under its name. It is a considerable
improvement on the AA (1908) definition of corporate entry.
The word 'implicitly' used twice in the CCR (1960) rule is
equivalent to 'avowed responsibility' in personal authorship.

Rule 26 deals with the related problem of personal
versus corporate entry, and again, quite specific and definite
guidance is given:

A work of an individual issued by a corporate body
is entered under the name of the individual,
except
(a) When the work is prepared for and issued in
the name of the corporate body.
(b) When the work represents an administrative,
regulatory, or official communication of a
corporate body, which may successively be
represented by different individuals.
(c) When the work represents an official
statement made by an individual on behalf
of a corporate body represented by him, or
as the spokesman of an office for which he
is responsible; an added entry is made under

the issuing body when the work is obviously
sponsored by it, but not when the work is
merely published by it.

Again, this rule gives reasonably precise instructions, and is
generally in accord with what we have previously stated, that
when both a personal and a corporate name are given on a
title-page, corporate entry must be proved, the balance being
in favour of personal entry. It is a rule based on title-page
data only, and the nature of the publication itself, and not on
extra-bibliographical considerations such as the financial
relationship between the personal author and the corporate
body. There is no comparable general statement in either
AA (1908) or ALA (1949). The latter does attempt some
guidance in rule 75C and D, limiting it to government
publications in terms of a report by an official or not by
an official. As we have already noted, this must be generalized
by the cataloguer himself for all other types of corporate body,
except for the rather backhanded statement in rule 71 — 'Monographic works by individual officers, members and employees
of corporate bodies, when these works are not clearly
administrative or routine in character, are preferably to be
entered under personal author, even though issued by a
corporate body'. This only refers to 'individual officers,
m embers and employees of corporate bodies', and makes no
direct reference to other persons who may not be in the same
position. The assumption is that the latters' publications
would be regarded as personal authorship. CCR (1960) not only
states this, but also shifts the emphasis from the relationship
of the person with the corporate body to the nature and status
of the publication itself.

Subordinate bodies are similarly treated according to
the bibliographical conditions of the title-page, where generally
the status of the 'name' of the body (whether self- sufficient in
itself, or indicating subordination) is taken as the criterion for
entry under the name of the subordinate body or the parent
organization in rules 23 and 33.

Government publications
The same simplifications are consistently applied to government
publications as to other types of corporate authorship.

103

CCR (1960) clearly defines what is to be regarded as a government publication, when both a personal and governmental body's name appear on a title-page, on the same lines as for other corporate bodies. The scope of government authorship is clearly defined as only to include the legislative, administrative, or judicial branches of government, and not governmental offices or agencies established to serve educational, cultural or scientific, etc functions (rule 47).

Some of the more controversial rules are those abolishing form headings for constitutions, treaties, and also for laws, statues, etc (rules 42, 42a, 42b). Constitutions and treaties are catered for by supplying a standardised *title* in square brackets in place of the form subdivisions of headings given in AA (1908) and ALA (1949). No such provision is given for laws, statues and the like, but presumably a similar filing title would be necessary to avoid the material being scattered under the name of the jurisdiction by the initial words of each title of each statute or law. The omission is due to the fact that CCR (1960) is an unfinished draft, and the rules for legal publications had not been formulated. The avoidance of form headings is consonant with the basic philosophy of the code that a work will be known and entered in the catalogue by a named author and a given title. Paul Dunkin, in his commentary adjoining this rule, maintains that this principle demands a complete separation of the author from the title element in the entry. The previous form divisions in headings, for example:

United States.   *Laws, statutes, etc.*

are compounded of both author and title elements, and are thus inadmissible in an author catalogue. So far as the user of the catalogue is concerned it might be argued that the change is one of style rather than of substance. In the two forms:

Great Britain. *Treaties*

and

Great Britain
Treaties

the order of the elements for filing is the same, but the form subheading will result in a convenient grouping of similar material, whereas the supplied standardised title will result in such entries being interfiled with other titles entered under the name of the jurisdiction only. While agreeing that form headings or subheadings should be kept to a minimum, this change would appear to have been introduced solely to preserve the consistency of the code, rather than to provide a more helpful heading in the catalogue. AACR (1967) reverts to the previous use of form headings, as in ALA (1949), for example:

Great Britain. *Laws, statutes, etc.*

Harvard Law School and the Main University Library did not consider the change 'a necessary one'.[1]

'Constitution' and 'treaties' are not quite the same as subheadings as 'Laws, statutes, etc'. The former two can be regarded as conventionalised titles, while the latter is merely a convenient subheading for bringing together a vast amount of diverse material in the form of laws, statutes, etc, and is the only true 'form' subheading of the three.

'Even though the present practice does not strictly adhere to the author-title principles of the new code, it [form subheadings] seems to be a legitimate exception inasmuch as experience shows that it makes the catalogue easier to use. It is difficult to see how the change would effect an improvement[2].

Summary of conclusions regarding CCR (1960)

Certain aspects of CCR (1960) make it unique, and may be summarized as follows:

1 It is the first attempt to construct a completely logical and consistent code of author/title rules, based on certain clearly stated principles of entry. Cutter's logic of the user is replaced by the logic of the code-maker. It avoids the exceptions found in ALA (1949) by confining itself to a set of rules for author and title entry, *ie* works are entered under author, if one is present, and under title if not. It does not admit any other type of entry, *eg* form or subject, which were both present to some extent in former codes. CCR (1960) also keeps the author element in the entry quite separate from the

1 Susan M Haskins. Is Harvard bound by the past? *Library resources* 5 (3) Summer 1961, 189-198.
2 David R Watkins. A reference librarian's view of the Draft cataloging code. *Library journal.* May 1 1961, 1730-1733.

title element; a work is described under the name of a known author, and given a particular title. At times, as we have just seen, this consistency is pursued at the expense of a more convenient heading in the catalogue.

2 Because the code returns to basic principles, it lists only the basic rules, leaving cataloguers to interpret the rules and apply them to specific problems and types of publication, guided by the logical consistency of the rules themselves.

3 It is a bibliographic code, recognising the importance of the title-page, and basing its rules on the conditions found thereon, rather than on extra-bibliographical criteria. This is, perhaps, one of its most important and influential features. A definition of author is not given. No principles of authorship are propounded. Criteria of authorship are based solely on title-page data. To this extent, it looks back to Panizzi's code.

4 It is a theoretical code, based on a logically consistent set of rules without regard to existing cataloguing practices based on previous codes. It ignores the alterations which would be necessary in the entries in actual catalogues in libraries to bring them into line with those constructed by its rules.

5 CCR (1960) avoids the making of subjective judgements on the part of cataloguers, which the earlier codes occasionally demanded. These subjective judgements were usually not based on title-page criteria, but on an examination of the whole work, with the result that the judgements were often bibliographically irrelevant.

Reaction to CCR (1960) was generally favourable.[1] Its basic principles and faultless logic could not but disarm much criticism and evoke general admiration. In general, cataloguers were enthusiastic; it has a cataloguers' code. When cataloguers did voice criticism, it was usually from the context of the cataloguing practices in their own libraries, and on the amount of alteration of existing entries which adoption of CCR (1960) would entail.

Reference librarians were less enthusiastic. They looked with nostalgia at the vast bio/bibliographic catalogues already built up, which had proved eminently suitable for answering easily and promptly many questions besides those of which library catalogues were supposedly designed to answer. They

1 *Library resources* 5 (3) Summer 1961 contains a series of articles on CCR (1960).

were also critical of the code's emphasis on 'differentiation' rather than 'identification' of bibliographic items![1]

Library administrators were in favour of the simplifications of CCR (1960) as they hinted at speedier and less costly cataloguing, while they were at the same time perturbed at the number of entries which would need to be altered in existing catalogues. The Association of Research Libraries and the Library of Congress were pessimistic at the quantitative effect altered headings would have, even if they represented only a very small percentage of the total number of the cards in their catalogues.[2, 3]

Particularly critical of CCR (1960) from the viewpoint of the needs of union catalogues was J L Dewton, Assistant Chief of the Union Catalog Division of the Library of Congress. He criticised the philosophic basis of the code, and its lack of detailed rules for specific cases, pointing out the variations in interpretation by cataloguers using ALA (1949), which spells our rules for specific problems, when contributing entries to the *National union catalog*.[4]

1 David R Watkins. *op cit*
2 Wyllis E Wright. Comparison of results of use of CCR draft code versus present ALA rules. *Library resources* 5 (3) Summer 1961, 186-198.
3 C Sumner Spalding. The quantitative effects of changed cataloging rules in the existing catalog. *Ibid*, 198-206.
4 Johannes L Dewton. The grand illusion: some observations on the present state of cataloging and the American Library Association's Draft code. *Library journal.* May 1 1961, 1719-1729.

10
ICCP, 1961

The International Conference on Cataloguing Principles was
held in Paris in October 1961.[1] The conference was one of the
most important events in the history of cataloguing during the
present century; it will be referred to hereafter as ICCP (1961).
It is doubtful if the conference would have had the success it
did have without CCR (1960) preceding it, when Lubetzky
persuaded the Americans to rationalise their cataloguing
practices. ALA (1949) would have been entirely unacceptable
as the basis for world-wide international agreement. But, while
the logic of CCR (1960) made the conference possible and
reasonably successful, the delegates by no means accepted all its
recommendations. That the conference was successful was also
due to the fact that only basic principles of author and title
cataloguing were discussed, and not details of rules based on
these principles. While it may be said that ICCP (1961) is
solely a statement of principles, and indeed its agreed statements
are called principles, quite a number of the so-called principles
are in effect closely detailed rules, for example, Principle 10,
for multiple authorship. What ICCP (1961) does is to attempt to
group under one all-pervasive rule a number of separate rules
dealing with similar problems which were a feature of the earlier
codes. The aim of the conference was to provide basic agreement
on principles to guide the framers of future national codes to   .
achieve a measure of international agreement. In their attempt
to achieve a good degree of unanimity the Steering Committee
were adroit in providing for alternatives, and also, very
occasionally, were purposely vague in their wording of certain
principles, so that it is difficult for any national committee to
1   *Op cit,* p 13.
108

to appreciate exactly what the principle is. For example, in corporate authorship there is a hidden disagreement as to whether corporate authors exist in their own right in catalogue headings or whether they are merely 'tags of convenience' to get round a difficulty. We shall return to this point later.

The conference had its origin in a meeting of the IFLA Cataloguing Rules Committee in 1954, and a special working group was set up, which reported to the International Congress of Libraries and Documentation Centres at Brussels in 1955. A preliminary meeting was held in London in 1959. Working papers were prepared by cataloguing experts on the main problem areas, and these were submitted to the national cataloguing committees to be discussed locally. On the basis of the original working papers and the comments received from the national committees a Draft Statement of Principles was drawn up, which was to serve as the starting-point of discussions at the conference.

Before considering the final statement of principles, it would be as well to look at the definition of Authorship included in the list of bibliographic terms accompanying the Principles. An author is defined as:

A person or corporate body who created a work or
is responsible for its intellectual content,
arrangement or form.

This definition may be compared to the lack of one in CCR (1960), and to the definitions of authorship in AA (1908) and ALA (1949) which it resembles closely. The definition clearly places ICCP (1961) on the side of those who hold to the intellectual responsibility concept of authorship. The definition is also sufficiently wide to include editorship and collectorship.

The functions of the catalogue are set out in the second Principle:

The catalogue should be an efficient instrument
for ascertaining:
2.1 whether the library contains a particular
book specified by
  (a) its author and title, *or*
  (b) if the author is not named in the book,
    its title alone, *or*
  (c) if the author and title are inappropriate

109

or insufficient for identification,
a suitable substitute for the title; and

2.2 (a)   which works by a particular author and
     (b)   which editions of a particular work are in
the library.

The above is a very broad statement of the functions of the author catalogue. 2.1 emphasises the single unit, while 2.2 emphasises the work rather than the single book. Some of the delegates regarded 2.2 as subordinate and less important than 2.1. The result of this disagreement will be seen when discussing later principles. 2.1 (c) would seem to suggest the use of form headings or at least standard titles, again, more of which later. Basically Principle 2 states the functions of the catalogue; it does not attempt to indicate how these functions should be carried out.. This was to give rise to disagreement, too. Principles 3 and 4 deal with the need for more than one entry, and their kinds.

Principle 5 is concerned with the use of multiple entries, and in effect says how the functions stated in Principle 2 are to be carried out.

5   Use of multiple entries
The two functions of the catalogue (see 2.1 and 2.2) are most efficiently discharged by

5.1   an entry for each book under a heading derived from the author's name or from the title as printed in the book, *and*

5.2   when variant forms of the author's name or of the title occur, an entry for each book under a *uniform heading,* consisting of one particular form of the author's name, or one particular title, or, for books not identified by author or title, a uniform heading consisting of a suitable substitute for the title, *and*

5.3   appropriate added entries and/or references.

Principle 5.1 is obviously linked with the functions of the catalogue stated in 2.1, and 5.2 with those in 2.2. Function 2.2 could have been satisfied by means other than

110

those suggested in 5.2, for example variant forms of an author's name or title of a work could have been entered as they stood, connected by references. This principle is included for completeness; what it does not state, and what is bound to be more controversial, is which of the entries mentioned in 5.1 and 5.2 should be the main entry. This follows in Principle 6, function of different kinds of entry. Summarised, the provisions are as follows:

6.1 The main entry for works entered under authors' names should normally be under a *uniform heading.* Main entries for works entered under title may be *either* under the title as printed in the book *or* under a uniform title with added entries or references under the other titles.

6.2 Entries under other names or forms of name for the same author should normally take the form of *references,* but added entries may be made in special cases.

6.3 Entries under other titles for the same work should normally take the form of added entries, but references may be used when they would take the place of numerous added entries.

Principle 6 evoked more comment from the delegates than almost any other principle. This is not surprising, considering the confusion of thought and inconsistencies revealed by it, especially 6.1. Agreement on the first part of 6.1 obviously indicates acceptance of the literary unit as a valid principle by the delegates. The alternatives allowed in the second part of 6.1 just as obviously indicate the lack of agreement as to the validity of the bibliographic unit. The Scandinavian countries – Denmark, Finland and Sweden, were the principal objectors, stating the view that the function of main entries in alphabetical catalogues should be to record *books* and not *works.* This again is the conflict between the collocative and the direct catalogue. It was also pointed out by other delegates, including Dr Osborn, that the use of a standard title following an author's name in the main entry introduced an element of filing, adding something that was not an essential part of the main entry, but could be regarded as filing information. This was outside the scope of the conference, and should be left for individual libraries to decide.

This statement has some validity, especially as the footnote to the principle indicates that the principles established for the treatment of works entered under title may also be applied in arranging entries under any particular author heading. Dr. Osborn was correct in suggesting that this was really outside the scope of the conference. Its presence was the unfortunate source of much irrelevant discussion. The same footnote also gave rise to considerable discussion about modern scientific and technical works, which in individual libraries may exist and be useful only in translation. The main principle would refer to such works only if they were anonymous (a small minority), but the footnote introduces the added problem of entering them under the title under their authors' names. In many circumstances the original title would be quite useless. The footnote would have been better omitted.

Principle 7 refers to the choice of a standard heading for personal authors, and indicates that this, when there are variant forms and names used by an author, should be the one most frequently used. This is outside the scope of the present paper.

The first seven sections of the Statement of Principles are general statements applicable to all types of publication, the remaining principles (8 to 12) are applicable to particular forms and types of publication.

Corporate authorship (Sections 9.1 – 9.3)
One of the results of the Paris conference which possibly characterised it more than any other was the majority acceptance of the principle that corporate bodies could be regarded as authors. The acceptance of this principle was regarded as a victory for the Anglo-American tradition over that of the German, Scandinavian and Middle-European practice of regarding all works issued by a corporate body (except certain private firms) as anonymous, if no personal name appeared on the title-page. It is ironic that Germany, the home of this tradition, was prepared to accept names of corporate bodies as headings 'in the interests of international unity', but that some of the countries which had followed the German practice were not, particularly Czechoslovakia, Denmark, Finland, Netherlands, Sweden and Yugoslavia. We will return later to their objections. France had officially adopted the principle of corporate
112

authorship eleven years earlier, and at the conference its delegates were particularly emphatic in their support of corporate authorship.

It was largely over the question of whether a corporate body could be considered an *author,* as opposed to being merely a useful and distinctive element in a title that trouble arose. This can be seen in the variation in the wording between the draft statement of principle and the final agreed version. The draft statement reads as follows:

9.1 *A corporate body* (i.e. any institution, organised body or assembly of persons known by a corporate or collective name) may be treated in the catalogue as the author of a work or serial publication.

In the final draft, the concept of a corporate body as an *author* is tacitly dropped:

9.1 The main entry for a work should be made under the name of a corporate body (i.e. any institution, organised body, or assembly of persons known by a collective or corporate name).

Here there is no mention of a corporate body as an *author.* All that is stated is that a main entry may be made under a corporate body. It is significant, also, that the first draft is headed *Corporate authors,* while the final statement is entitled *Entry under corporate bodies.*

While this concession may have been made to secure majority agreement, it is in conflict with the concept of authorship as inferred and agreed upon in the preceding principles, and is also at variance with the definition of authorship already quoted from the principles (See p.109. Section 9.1 in its revised form is also so wide that various concepts of corporate authorship can be included under its umbrella.

The two subsections of 9.1 indicate the circumstances in which publications of corporate bodies may have entry under the name of the body:

9.11 When the work is by its nature necessarily the expression of the collective thought or activity of the corporate body, even if by a person in the capacity of an officer or servant of the corporate body.

This subsection would seem to support those who regard corporate

113

bodies as authors, but the following subsection would seem to favour the view that the name of a corporate body is merely a distinctive and useful title-tag:

9.12 When the wording of the title or the title-page, taken in conjunction with the nature of the work clearly implies that the corporate body is collectively responsible for the content of the work. *Footnote:* e.g. serials whose titles consist of a generic term (Bulletin, Transac-.tion, etc.) preceded or followed by the name of the corporate body, and which include some account of the activities of the body.

The footnote would seem to point to entry under a corporate body because its name is the only part of the title of such a publication which is distinctive and memorable. We have two distinct principles at work here — corporate body as author, and the name of the corporate body as the sole distinctive element in certain titles. Of the two subsequent codes, AA (1967) favours the first interpretation, while the 1965 rules of the Verein Deutscher Bibliothekare state that a corporate body which is the originator of a work may only have entry if:

a the work is anonymous, *ie* does not contain the name of a personal author.

b the name of the corporate body is included in the title of the work or the work cannot be properly named without it.

The German code obviously subscribes to the identification tag concept of corporate authorship, and this by a country whose delegates accepted the principle of corporate authorship as stated in section 9.

The next section, 9.2 states the circumstances when a corporate body would not have main entry:

9.2 In other cases when a corporate body has performed a function (such as that of an editor) subsidiary to the function of an author, an *added* entry should be made under the name of the corporate body.

Here the concept of *authorship* is again introduced, and its absence made the criterion for avoiding corporate entry for main entry. This is inconsistent with the 'identification tag'

114

role of corporate authorship stated in 9.12.

9.3 deals with doubtful cases where the main entry may be under personal author, corporate body or title, at the discretion of the cataloguer, with added entries under the elements not chosen for the main entry. This would appear to beg the whole question.

The acceptance of corporate bodies as authors appears as a victory for the Anglo-American tradition, but the concessions which had to be made render the compromise virtually meaningless. The idea of the name of a corporate body as a convenient heading was accepted by some of the delegates, but others representing such countries as Sweden, Denmark and Finland could not even accept his interpretation, regarding the whole practice of using corporate names as headings as too complicated and impractical. They were prepared to make entries under the name of a corporate body for anonymous works issued by it, provided its name formed the only distinctive element in the title. All others would be treated as anonymous. This is not entry under a corporate body as an author, but title entry under the most significant word in the title. They were also prepared to accept that added entries be made for all corporate bodies whose names formed part of the title of a publication. The Czechoslovak delegation were only prepared to accept corporate author headings as references. Their reasons were:

1   The difficulty of establishing the correct heading.

2   If corporate names were used for main headings, the structure of the catalogue would be further complicated by the need to distinguish between three different types of heading.

3   Whenever the name of a corporate body changed it would be more economical if only a reference had to be altered, not the main entries.

4   Uniformity would not be achieved if corporate bodies were to have main entry because these often had to be given in different languages for the convenience of the users.

All these objections, with the exception of the second, are not objections to the principle of corporate authorship, but rather to the practical difficulties which ensue once corporate author headings have been accepted.

115

Multiple authorship
Multiple authorship, as distinct from corporate authorship, is
dealt with in the next section (section 10). The scope of the
principle is extremely wide, since no distinction is made
between differentiated and undifferentiated multiple
authorship, as in the previous codes. In general, section 10 follows
CCR (1960) fairly closely. It runs as follows:
> When two or more authors have shared in the
> creation of a work,
>
> 10.1   When one author is represented in the book
> as the principal author, the others playing a
> subordinate or subsidiary role, the main
> entry for the work should be made under
> the name of the principal author;
>
> 10.2   If no author is represented as the principal
> author, the main entry should be made under
>
> 10.21   the author first named on the title-page, if
> the number of authors is two or three, added
> entries being made under the name(s) of the
> other author(s),
>
> 10.22   the title of the work, if the number of authors
> is more than three, added entries being made
> under the author named first in the book and
> under as many other authors as may appear
> necessary.

The scope of this section is very wide, covering all types of
multiple authorship, except collections. It includes joint
authorship, composite works, revisions, translations, adaptations,
etc. The contributions of the different persons need not be of
the same type, also included are illustrated works, and music with
wods.[1]

It may be questioned whether one omnibus rule is adequate
to cover all types of multiple authorship. To illustrate the point,
consider the following work written by two authors, and revised
by another three:
> Spicer and Pegler's/Book-Keeping/and accounts/
> Sixteenth edition/by/W.W.Bigg, F.C.A./H.A.R.J.
> Wilson, F.C.A./and/A.E.Langton, Ll.B.(Lond), F.C.A./...

---

1 International Conference on Cataloguing Principles. Statement of principles;
annotated ed, by A H Chaplin, assisted by Dorothy Anderson, London, 1966.

As there are five authors in all, and no *one* is represented as the principal author, entry must be made under the title, which would certainly be inappropriate for this book. The root of the trouble would seem to lie in the lack of any distinction between undifferentiated and differentiated multiple authorship.

The statement also suffers from other faults. The emphasis is on one principal author as represented in the book, not on the title-page, and therefore does not cover those instances where the order of citing the contributors on the title-page may differ from the order in which they appear in the book. AACR (1967) covers this point in rule 3, where the order of the title-page is preferred As in CCR (1960) the role of the editor is ignored. As some of the delegates also pointed out, the rule is not particularly useful in the case of modern scientific and technical papers written by a number of authors as a result of group research, and which are known by the names of their authors.

Section 10.3 deals with collections. The same distinction is made as in ALA (1949) rule 5 and in rule 4 of CCR (1960) between collections of works which have had a previous independent existence, and composite works consisting of specially written contributions for the volume concerned. The latter are included in 10. The treatment of collections caused a difference of opinion at the conference, the delegates being almost equally divided between two alternatives for the main entry. The majority were in favour of entry under uniform title unless the name of the compiler appears prominently on the title-page; while a large minority were in favour of entry under the compiler, if he is named on the title-page. The first has the merit of consistency of entry with other works by more than three authors, if no one is represented as the principal author. This type of collection, in which the works of the various authors have probably been arbitrarily brought together by the compiler, is even less likely to be remembered by the names of the individual authors. The second alternative, on the other hand, recognises that the compiler of such a collection, especially if it is of literary material, has produced a unique work. Often such literary anthologies are known by the names of their compilers, for example Sir Francis Palgrave's *Golden treasury*.

117

However, the difference between the two alternatives is more apparent than real because of the concessions which each makes to the other. The number of collections where the two rules would not coincide must be small, and as added entries are to be made under the element not chosen for the main entry in each alternative, the final result is similar.

Form headings and subheadings

Section 12 of the draft statement of principles allowed the use of form headings and subheadings for certain categories of material. 12.1 recommended that a certain limited number of categories of books, consisting of items which are usually anonymous and issued either without titles or with descriptive titles which are similar in meaning for each category, though varying in wording, and which cannot readily be identified by author and title should be given form of entry. The main entry for such books should be made under form headings, indicating the category to which such books belong, for example sale catalogues, diaries and calendars, theatre programmes, political leaflets and posters, etc. Considerable latitude was to be left to individual countries as to the exact contents of such categories. It was also suggested that a list of such categories of material might be drawn up. 12.2 also suggested that books which have an author (personal or corporate) should have their main entry under their author's name followed by a form subheading — laws and treaties under the names of states, and under personal authors such form subdivisions as single letters, speeches, etc. Both draft statements aroused considerable discussion. The CCR (1960) position, which denied the validity of such form headings or subheadings in an author/title catalogue was defended by Lubetzky, but the majority of the delegates were in favour of the introduction of some form headings, if only as a practical necessity. Form subheadings under personal authors were rejected as internal library filing devices outwith the scope of the conference. Finally a section was added to statement 9 that constitutions, laws and other works of similar characteristics should be entered under the name of the state or other territory with formal or conventional *titles* indicating the nature of the material. To this extent Lubetzky persuaded the delegates, as this use of conventional titles rather than form subheadings is the position of CCR (1960). The objections to this have already been discussed

118

in relation to CCR (1960). While treaties and constitutions could be subsumed under conventional titles, the same can hardly be said of laws, etc, a term which would indicate a type of material rather than a substitute for a title.

Form headings are allowed by statement 11.6 for multilateral treaties and conventions, and other categories of publication (unspecified) issued with non-distinctive titles. A resolution passed by the conference proposed a 'restricted list' of such categories of publications, but so far no such list has been published. See Resolution IVA2 (c):

A restricted list of categories of publications
which may be entered under a conventional
heading reflecting the form of the work. .[1]

The significance of the ICCP principles
The principles of author/title cataloguing, agreed at Paris in 1961 were undoubtedly significant in the history of cataloguing. Nothing quite like them had happened before. They are the culmination of twenty years of intensive debate initiated by Andrew Osborn in 1941, and continued by Lubetzky in 1953 and 1960. One valuable aspect of the conference was that it involved Europe, and, indeed, the rest of the world as well as the Americans. It brought the Anglo-American and German-Central European cataloguing traditions face to face. One might have expected a new synthesis of cataloguing theory and principles to emerge. It is one of the disappointing features of the conference that this new alchemy did not occur. The German and European libraries had suffered much during the war, and after cessation of hostilities during the reconstruction period they were so subjected to American influences that they had little in the way of cohesive alternatives to offer. Where genuine differences did occur the final agreed statements of many of the principles are so hedged round with permissive phrases and alternatives that more than one interpretation can be taken out of them. We have already seen that two subsequent codes have interpreted the rule for corporate authorship differently. This is a serious situation for a code of principles whose primary function was to achieve basic international uniformity in all subsequent national codes. Like many post-war international

1 ICCP Report, p 97.

conferences, and in spite of the glossary of terms in five languages appended to the statement, one has the feeling that the term is interpreted differently by different delegations.

The final statement of principles also illustrates, in many instances, a desire to achieve agreement rather than to enunciate a clear, precise rule or principle. But, however open to various interpretations the principles are, they cannot be ignored. They place all subsequent national codes and revisions of codes in an international context. The editor of AACR (1967) is at pains to state that it follows the 'Paris principles', with a few exceptions which are then detailed.[1]

The ICCP principles evoked surprisingly little comment in the professional journals. This may be due to the fact that little else can be said after twenty years of debate. It may also be attributable to the principles themselves, being all things to all men, and allowing so diverse interpretations that whatever one's views on the basic principles of author/title cataloguing one can find little to argue about.

1 Anglo-American cataloguing rules (American text). Introduction, pp 2-5.

11
ANGLO-AMERICAN CATALOGUING RULES, 1967

January 1967 saw the publication of the long-awaited new Anglo-American cataloguing rules in the United States, referred to hereafter as AACR (1967)[1] The British text was not published until the end of the same year[2] The two texts have been published in different formats in the two countries. Like AA (1908), there are differences between the two texts, but unlike the earlier code, the differing readings of rules are not printed together. The British text gives the American alternative rules for entry and headings in Appendix VI in full, whereas the North American text merely gives the numbers of the rules where their British colleagues disagreed with them in Appendix 6. Like its predecessors of 1908 and 1949, AACR (1967) contains rules designed primarily for the needs of large research livraries. 'These rules have been drawn up primarily to respond to the needs of general research libraries' (*Intro*, p 1). The needs of smaller and less scholarly libraries are, however, taken into account by the provision of alternatives where their needs conflict with those of the large research library, by allowing, for example, an author to be entered under his different pseudonyms. The editor also makes the point that because considerable emphasis has been placed on providing more direct headings, and because the headings themselves have been simplified, this in itself should make the code more attractive to smaller, more popular libraries.

The rules themselves derive from the Paris Principles, which, in turn, owe much to the work of Seymour Lubetzky. Seymour

1 American Library Association. Anglo-American cataloging rules (American text). Chicago, 1967.
2 Library Association. Anglo-American cataloguing rules (British text). London, 1967

121

Lubetzky acted as editor of the code from 1956 to 1962, and the work was completed by C Sumner Spalding from 1963 to 1966. The ALA Catalog Code Revision Committee adopted the Paris Principles with certain reservations in 1962. Shortly after, the Library of Congress made a study of the theoretical merits of the Paris Principles, and more particularly, of the changes which would be necessary in the entries in its catalogues if the principles were to be adopted in their entirety. The Association of Research Libraries supported the Library of Congress in its conclusion that certain provisions of the Paris Principles be reconsidered, in particular Principle 9.4, which recommended entry under name for all corporate bodies. Rules 98 and 99 of the North American text make exception to entry under name in favour of entry under place for certain specified types of corporate body. This exception was not taken up by the British Committee, who accepted ICCP 9.4. The other deviations from the ICCP Principles are more minor, and will be dealt with later.

Following Lubetzky's influence and example, the structure of the code is built on basic rules to cover conditions of authorship rather than presenting a proliferation of specific rules to cover types of publication. 'The rules are framed round an analysis of the various patterns in which this responsibility may be distributed between persons, between corporate bodies, and between persons and corporate bodies'.[1] Special rules there are, but these are always to be regarded within the context of the more general, basic rules.

AACR (1967) consistently separates the problems of entry from those of the construction and form of heading. Part I is concerned with entry and heading, Part II with description, and Part III with rules for certain specified types of non-book material, insofar as they need different or supplementary rulings to those for book materials. Again, within Part II the rules for entry and heading are kept quite separate from those for description.

Part I, chapter 1: Rules for entry
Unlike ICCP (1961) or CCR (1960) this code regrettably does not set out a list of objectives for the author-title catalogue,

1   Anglo American Cataloguing rules (American text), p

but acceptance of those stated in ICCP (1961) is implicit in the Introduction. This is all the more regrettable after Lubetzky's emphasis on the value of a clearly defined set of principles in the construction of a code of rules for author cataloguing. The only ICCP principles which are stated are those which were not accepted. This makes AACR (1967) incomplete in itself.

AACR (1967) still adheres to the distinction between main and added entries. 'The rules in this chapter are primarily rules for determining the main entry of a work. "Enter under" is to be interpreted as "make main entry under . . . ' (p 9) At the end of the chapter on Entry there is a section dealing with the circumstances under which added entries are to be made (rule 33), apart from specific instructions to make added entries with particular rules.

The choice of main entry is determined by the criterion of authorship stated in the code as a footnote to p 9:

By 'author' is meant the person or corporate body chiefly responsible for the creation of the intellectual or artistic content of a work. Thus composers, artists, photographers, etc. are the 'authors' of the works they create; chess players are the 'authors' of their recorded games; etc. The term 'author' also embraces an editor or compiler who has primary responsibility for the content of a work, e.g. the compiler of a bibliography.

Thus AACR (1967) continues the tradition of 'intellectual responsibility' as the primary criterion of authorship. But it puts limits on the application of the principle by stating that entry for a work is normally based on the statements that appear on the title-page or on any part of the work used as its substitute. Material appearing elsewhere in the book is only to be used for the determination of the main entry when the information on the title-page is ambiguous or insufficient. Sources outside the work itself are only to be used in the case of anonymous works, or where there is doubt as to the authenticity of statements made in the publication itself.[1] Thus, the concept of intellectual responsibility is considerably modified by making the title-page the primary source for the heading. This, roughly, was the position of Lubetzky and

1   Anglo-American Cataloguing rules (British text) p 9.

CCR (1960) and contrasts with the acceptance of the concept of intellectual responsibility without the restraints of the title-page as in ALA (1949). It goes back to Lubetzky's emphasis on the bibliographical condition that most modern books have title-pages whose function is to identify the book.

While the main entry's function is to enter under the person or body judged to be responsible for the intellectual content of a work, the function of added entries is 'to provide additional direct access to bibliographic items that are represented in the catalogue' (p 58). Added entries are usually considered to have two principal functions:

1 To provide access to material in the catalogue under headings other than that chosen for the main entry.

2 To complete the bibliographical record in the catalogue of a person's or corporate body's output.

The second function is not catered for by the instructions for added entries in AACR (1967). 'If it is desired that the catalogue shall display fully the significant bibliographical activities of each person or corporate body, insofar as these are represented by works that have been catalogued, it will be necessary to go beyond these rules' (p 59).

Like all previous codes, the first choice of entry is the author or principal author when one can be determined. If there is no author or principal author, then an editor who is primarily responsible for a work is the next choice, followed by a compiler of a collection, if named on the title-page. Title entry is to be used for those works whose authorship is 'diffuse, indeterminate, or unknown'. The only other form of heading which is admissible is a form heading for certain types or forms of work. The term 'principal author' is a new concept which did not appear in either AA (1908) or ALA (1949). It is defined in rule 3A as 'The person or corporate body, if any, to whom the principal responsibility is attributed, e.g. by wording or typography'.

The evidence of the title-page is not taken as conclusive so far as determination of authorship is concerned. The first rule in the code states:

1A Enter a work, a collection of works, or
       selections of works by one author under
       the person or corporate body that is the

author, *whether named in the work or not.*
Similarly in rule 1B:

1B   If the publication attributes authorship
     erroneously or fictitiously to someone
     who is not the author, *enter it under the
     actual author* and make an added entry
     under the person to whom authorship is
     attributed if he is a real person.

In spite of what has been stated previously about the importance
of title-page information, so far as authorship is concerned, the
title-page is not sufficient evidence. There might be some difficulty
in interpretation between rule 1B and rule 42 for pseudonyms
which allows entry under pseudonym, though the point is
reasonably clear that, because rules for entry are kept quite
distinct from those for form of heading, rule 42 refers to
pseudonyms used by real persons. This departure from the
title-page as the source for the heading is necessary in this case.
If one were to establish author headings solely on information
found on the title-page of the works being catalogued or elsewhere
within them, one could have the separation of entries for different editions of the same work if some were published anonymously, and some with their authors' names, a situation which,
as we have seen, can arise with the British Museum rules, except in
the case of the recognised 'classics'. Nor can the evidence of the
title-page be taken as conclusive if the distinction between the
'work' and the 'book' or 'edition' referred to in Chapter 1 is to
be recognised. AACR (1967) is based on the recognition of the
'work' as the unit of author cataloguing, and not the 'book'.
The statements of the rules in the first section of the code
carefully use the word 'work' and not 'book'.

   AACR (1967) defines an anonymous work as 'a work of
unknown authorship'. There is no mention in the definition
of the distinction between an author's name appearing on the
title-page or elsewhere in a book. The writer would interpret
the definition as 'not known to the cataloguer' or 'not
discovered or discoverable by him'. What might appear to be a
curious omission in the case of an anonymous work whose
author is known, and which would consequently be entered
under the name of the author, is that, with the rule (2A),
there is no mention of an added entry under the title to
125

help those catalogue users who may not have the knowledge of the cataloguer. It is however covered by section P of rule 33 – 'Make a title added entry for every work of known authorship that is published anonymously'. This is a special case of added entry and should have been dealt with alongside the rule to which it refers, rather than with the general rule for added entries.

The definition of 'anonymous work', *ie* 'of unknown authorship' does not describe the condition of the work itself, but the knowledge of the cataloguer. This may be compared with the definition found with rule 32 in ALA (1949) – 'A strictly anonymous work is one in which the author's name does not appear anywhere in the book. AACR (1967) has the better definition because in neither code is a work treated as anonymous by the cataloguer if he knows the name of its author. It is only when this information is not known that the rules for anonymity apply. AACR (1967) is also more logical than its predecessor since it includes in the one rule both works whose authors are known and those whose authors are discovered, and does not separate the latter into a rule of their own. Anonymous works, by the definition stated above, are dealt with separately in the following rule: Rule 2: *Works of unknown or Uncertain authorship or by unnamed groups:*

Enter under title (or designation in lieu of title – see 103) a work that is of unknown or uncertain authorship, or that is by a group that lacks a name. Make added entries or author-title references under the names of persons to whom authorship has been attributed, either in editions of the work or in reference sources.

The North American text of this rule is worded differently:

Enter under title a work that is of unknown or uncertain authorship, or that is by a group that lacks a name. Make added entries under as many as three persons to whom authorship has been attributed, either in editions of the work or in reference sources. Always make an added entry under a person to whom authorship is attributed in the edition being catalogued.

The British text is more comprehensive. There is no mention of designation in lieu of title, though the North American text contains rule 103. It also limits added entries to three for persons to whom authorship has been attributed, but gives no indication as to which three, if more than three.

The inclusion in the anonymous category of publications by groups which lack names is in sharp contrast to ALA (1949) which supplied names to un-named corporate bodies (rules 140 and 141). These supplied names or descriptions were bibliographically irrelevant.

Pseudonymous works are treated in the section on Headings for Persons (rule 42) since it is the name or form of name which is under consideration, and not the author concerned.

Rules 1 and 2 deal with single authorship, while the next sixteen rules cover conditions of multiplicity of authorship, though there is a unifying thread in the concept of principal authorship applied to multiple authorship.

Multiple authorship

AACR (1967) recognises the distinction in multiple authorship between those works in which the authors have performed a similar function — *Works of shared authorship* (rules 3-6) and those in which different persons have performed different authorship functions — *Works with authorship of mixed character* (rules 7-18), a long section which includes corporate authorship. In making this distinction, AACR (1967) differs from ICCP (1961) but follows its other predecessors, notably CCR (1960) and ALA (1949).

In general, the first section follows closely the similar section of CCR (1960), including joint authorship, specially written contributions by a number of writers (composite works), and works consisting of an exchange between different persons, *ie* correspondence, debates, etc. Like CCR (1960), emphasis is on principal author, *rule 3A:*

Enter a work of shared authorship under the
person or corporate body, if any, to whom
principal responsibility is attributed, e.g.
by wording or typography.

Rules 3B1 & 2 cover situations where principal responsibility is not indicated. Here, as before, the rule of three applies. If there are not more than three authors, entry is under the first-named
127

(rule 3B1); rule 3B2 states that if more than three authors are involved, entry is under the title, unless the work has been produced under editorial direction, and the editor is named on the title-page. In this case rule 4 applies (works produced under editorial direction).

An examination of AACR (1967) rules 3 and 4 for Shared authorship, and for works produced under editorial direction gives no explicit guidance on the problem presented by the presence of an editor, *and* authors sharing in the production of a work. Rule 4 runs as follows:

Enter a work produced under editorial direction under its editor providing: 1) he is named on the title-page of the work, 2) the publisher is not named in the title, and 3) the editor appears to be primarily responsible for the existence of the work. In all other cases enter under the title and make an added entry under the editor if he is named on the title-page. If authors are named on the title-page, make an added entry under the one named first.

The wording of this rule does not make it clear whether the last sentence refers to the complete rule or only to the last part of the rule,(*ie* if entry is not made under the editor, but under the title). If the first interpretation is correct, then rule 4 becomes paramount, and takes precedence over rule 3, which is not in line with the general framework of AACR (1967). If the second interpretation is the correct one, then it contradicts rule 3B1 (where there are no more than three sharing authors and entry would be made under the first), and is redundant in terms of 3B2 which legislates for title entry anyway. Because of these inherent contradictions with the second interpretation, one must conclude that the first interpretation is the correct one. We thus have an order of priority: 1) Editor, if named on the title-page, etc; 2) Principal author; 3) First of two or three authors with no designation of principal responsibility; 4) Title, if more than three authors, without designation of principal responsibility. The stipulation in rule 4 that entry is not made under the editor when a publisher is named in the title, in which case title entry would prevail, gives rise to two curious examples to the rule. The examples are:

Entry under editor:
Directory of American scholars, a biographical
directory; edited by Jacques Cattell . . . 1942.
Entry under title:
Directory of American scholars, a biographical
directory; edited by the Jacques Cattell Press.
4th ed. . . . 1963.

Presumably the later edition is entered under its title because of
the provisions of rule 4 whereby entry is under title when a
publisher is named in the title. Such a practice, however,
contravenes the principle of treating the work as the unit.
Surely the two editions above are editions of the same 'work', and
should be entered together in the catalogue. The reason why
this has happened is pointed out by Lubetzky. [1] It arises from
the absence of a rule for 'Works of changing authorship' which
was present in CCR (1960) (see p 97). One must therefore treat
this category of work by the rule for serials (rule 6).

The provision for entry under editor if named on the title-
page is not part of the ICCP Principle (section 10.22). The preference for a named editor rather than title is generally in the
Anglo-American tradition of regarding a personal name as more
distinctive and worthy of entry than a title. The principal
criterion is inclusion on the title-page, and not primarily the
amount of editorial work executed, as in AA (1908). This avoids
subjective assessments on the part of the cataloguer, and results
in more sought headings.

This difference of opinion over choice of editor or title is
consistent with the rule for collections in AACR (1967) and
ICCP (1961). Collections of previously independent works are
covered in the two codes by rules 5 and 10.3 respectively. By
the former, collections published under a collective title are to be
entered under a compiler mentioned on the title-page, whereas
the majority decision at ICCP was in favour of title entry.
Underlying the difference is the more basic problem of how far
the functions of authorship can be carried over to those of an
editor or compiler, but the stipulation in AACR (1967) that the
compiler or editor must be named as such on the title-page again
seems to indicate that the prominence of a personal name on a title-
page was the overriding consideration. This, however, is more

1   Allen, Thelma E and Dickman, Daryl Ann. New rules for an old game.
London, 1968, pp. 62-63.

akin to cataloguing according to the most prominent feature of a title-page rather than on the principle of intellectual or artistic responsibility.

The multiple authorship group of rules in AACR (1967) also includes serials, *ie* publications issued in successive parts bearing numerical or chronological designations and intended to be continued indefinitely. Serials are to include periodicals, newspapers, journals and memoirs, proceedings and transactions of societies, annuals, and also monographic series. It may seem a little surprising to find a rule for *serials* in AACR (1967) because this is a type of publication rather than a condition of authorship. The presence of the rule is made necessary by the absence in AACR (1967) of a more general rule covering the bibliographic condition of changing authorship or editorship previously referred to. The main provision for serials has not changed, *ie* they are to be entered under their titles; what is different is the section of the rule dealing with serials issued by corporate bodies. The choice of entry — under title or corporate body — is now determined almost entirely from the title of the serial, and not, as formerly, on whether or not the serial contained only the regular proceedings, transactions, etc of the corporate body, an assessment that was extremely difficult to make. Generally, serials issued by corporate bodies are to be entered under their titles, and are only to be entered under the corporate body if either: 1) the title includes the name of the corporate body, or an abbreviation of it, or the title of an appropriate official; or 2) the title consists solely of a generic term or phrase which does not adequately identify the serial except when it is taken in conjunction with the name of the body. This is a much more satisfactory rule than that of AA (1908), being based solely on the *title,* and not on the contents of the serial. The wordings of the British and North American texts for serials vary in emphasis, the British text is more positive than the North American, while the latter also has a residual clause favouring entry under the corporate body in cases of doubt. The difference in the wording of the two texts would result in the Americans having more entries for such serials under corporate bodies than would the British text. There is also a new provision in both texts for a serial of which one person is the author or principal author, or which is the result of collaboration between two or three authors; entry
130

would be according to rules 1-3.

Differentiated multiple authorship
The section in AACR (1967) dealing with this type of authorship
is entitled 'Works with authorship of mixed character' (rules 8 to
18), but covers much the same material to that which we have
called 'Works of differentiated multiple authorship', *ie* where more
than one person is involved in the writing of a work, but in
different capacities, as author, or adapter, illustrator, translator,
etc. As in the previous codes, the primary criterion for the
determination of the main entry heading is that of intellectual
responsibility — 'assigning the main entry to the person or body
judged to be principally responsible for the intellectual or
artistic content of the work' (p 24). This is the primary
criterion, though in certain circumstances other criteria are invoked,
such as the prominence given to the different contributions on
the title-page, or even the order in which they are mentioned in
the title, *cf* rule 8 — Artist or author of the text.

The intellectual effort of adapting a work from one literary
style or form to another, *eg* writing for children, is sufficient for
authorship according to rule 7, which enters such adaptations
under the name of the adapter, and not that of the original author,
as in AA (1908) and ALA (1949). Even if the adapter is not
named on the title-page, entry does not go under the original
author, but under the title of the adaptation. The example
quoted is of an anonymous adaptation of the *Pilgrim's progress*
for the young. This would be given main entry under title, with
an added author/title entry under Bunyan. Given that this may
be the theoretically correct solution in terms of authorship or its
absence, it is of little utility in single-entry catalogues, such as
union catalogues, where different editions of the work by
anonymous adapters would be scattered according to the wording
of their title-pages. This throws some doubt on the wisdom of
regarding the adapter as being primarily responsible for such a
work. In this instance, the other criterion of 'Name most
permanently associated with a work' would be more suitable.

The rules for illustrated works follow the pattern of entry under
the person primarily responsible, the author or artist — rules 8B
and 8D, but a new category is introduced by rule 8A, that of the
collaborative work between author and artist. 8A refers to a work
131

planned as a cohesive whole, where entry is made under the contributor who is mentioned first on the title-page, unless the second is given considerably greater prominence, for example:

Architecture/ of the/ California Missions/
Text by/ Kurt Baer/ Photography by Hugo
Rudinger/

This ruling again leans heavily on the manner in which the information is set out on the title-page, but seems preferable to the attempt to assess the relative importance of the contributions, and is in line with the general practice of the code. It is in accord with the rule for multiple authorship where generally, the first name on the title-page is taken for the heading, when the volume comprises contributions specially written for the volume, and not having a previously independent existence. It is also in accord with the way in which the work is likely to be cited.

The principle of primary responsibility can account for rules 9, Biographer/critic or author; 10, Calligrapher or author; 11, Commentator or author; 12, Praeses or respondent in academic dissertations; 14, Reviser or original author; and 16, Writer or nominal author. Given this principle, the rules are not necessary. Rule 13 presents a different criterion of authorship. It deals with the problem of entry under person reported or under the reporter. The report of an interview or discussion, or similar exchange between persons is to be entered under the reporter, if he is a participant in the exchange, or if the report is mainly in his words. By rule 13B, however, if the reporter is not a participant and the report is confined to the words of the person or persons reported, entry is under the principal participant, the first-named, or title, as the case may be, according to rule 3. In certain circumstances, the criterion is the name most prominent on the title-page when that of principal responsibility is not applicable.

The section of AACR (1967) on *Works of mixed character* also deals with the problem of corporate versus personal authorship in rule 17. The provisions of rule 17 are similar to rules 22 and 26 of CCR (1960) if stated in different words. Again, the choice is determined by the primary responsibility for the work, and whether or not it represents the official views or policy of the corporate body, or is a statement of the personal

132

opinions, views, etc of the single author.

17A1: *Works of corporate authorship*
Enter under the corporate body, with an added
entry under the personal author or the one
named first, a work that is by its nature
necessarily the expression of the corporate
thought or activity of the body. Such
works include official records and reports, and
statements, studies and other communications
dealing with the policies, operations, or
management of the body made by officers or
other employees of the body. Single reports,
however, that are made by officers or other
employees that embody the results of
scholarly investigation or scientific
research are excluded unless written by more
than three persons, none of whom is represented
as the principal author. All reports and
studies prepared by consultants engaged for
the particular purpose are excluded.

Similarly rule 17B deals with the instances where entry would
not be under the name of the corporate body:-

Works not of corporate authorship
If the work would not be entered under
corporate body under the provisions of A
above, or if there is doubt as to whether it
would, enter it under the heading under
which it would be entered if no corporate
body were involved. Make an added entry
under the body unless it functions solely
as publisher.

These two rules follow what Lubetzky had stated in CCR (1960),
and also what had been stated in ICCP (1961). The types of
publication to be entered under a corporate body are clearly
detailed, and 17B makes it clear that in cases of doubt personal
authorship is to be preferred. What is new is the part of 17A
which allows entry of reports by more than three persons to be
made under the name of the corporate body, provided none is
represented as the principal author. This again ties up with the
rule for works of multiple authorship. This is suggested in AA
133

(1908) and ALA (1949), though the number of three authors is not specified. By relating the rule for corporate authorship to that for multiple authorship, AACR (1967) also emphasises the unity of the general problem, and does not treat works of corporate authorship as an isolated case. The rule also confirms that entry is made under the corporate body for works within the field in which the corporate body is interested, but not for material on other subjects. Rule 17A clears up the 'paid official' concept of entry which has been alluded to. There is however a certain element of subject entry involved in the distinction between entry under the corporate body or the official of the body. This subject element, which is alien to an author catalogue, is seen also in rule 17A2:

> Enter under the corporate body a work, other
> than a formal history, describing the body,
> its functions, procedures, facilities,
> resources, etc., or an inventory, catalogue,
> directory of personnel, list of members, etc.

Rule 17B also introduces a new factor which was not present in the CCR (1960) rule. In the latter code corporate authorship is allowed, except for commercial publishers, when a work is issued by a corporate body without the name of the personal author or compiler and not represented as an anonymous work (rule 22C). This practice represents a common method of treating the corporate body as author because it is the only name on the title-page.

Subordinate units of corporate bodies are to have entry when authorship is specifically and prominently attributed to them (rule 18). Assuming that the term 'prominently' refers to the title-page, this rule can be taken as another example of the choice of heading being based on the manner in which the information is stated on the title-page, rather than on such extra-bibliographical considerations as the relationship between the parent and the subordinate body. None of the rules on corporate authorship in this section of the code concern themselves with the name or form of name to be used for the corporate body. This is outwith this section of the code and is not relevant to the present paper, though it is one of the sections of AACR (1967) where the two committees differed considerably. Nor does this section deal with the question of

134

whether a subordinate body is to be entered directly under its own name or under the name of a parent or higher body. This again, is a question of form of name and is dealt with in the appropriate place in the code.

Government publications are not treated as such in the section on Entry in AACR (1967) – logically, as the main problem is the *form* of heading, *ie* entry under the governmental unit or the name of the body or organisation. Therefore, although not stated, the foregoing rules for choice between personal and corporate entry would also apply to government publications.

Related works
Related works are covered by rule 19. Certain types of related works have already been dealt with – adaptations, revisions, etc. These are works closely related to the works from which they derive their meaning; with the exception of adaptations their very names imply subordination to something else. A revision is a version of the original work. Similarly, the process of translation is not a creative process, but the rendering into another language of the results of the intellectual activity of someone else. If a measure of original creativity is also involved, then the work ceases to be a translation but becomes a work in its own right, as AACR (1967) recognises in rule 15 – 'If the translation involves adaptation, or is described as a free translation, however, treat it as an adaptation', *ie* enter it under its own author. The related works covered by rule 19B are related in a much looser manner to their parent works. They are not versions of earlier works, but works based upon previous works, and represent the creative intellectual activity of their own authors, for example concordances, supplements, continuations. Such are to be entered under their own authors. The intellectual responsibility criterion is obviously in action here. Rule 19A, however, lists exceptions to independent entry, for example, related works which have indistinctive titles or titles which are dependent on other works. These are to have entry under the works to which they relate. All others are treated as independent works, with the optional exception of librettos for particular musical compositions, which are to be entered under the composer/title of the musical work. This ruling is not based on intellectual responsibility, but rather on
135

the concept of the inseparable work, or even on that of the name most permanently associated with the work. The whole question is rather confused by the further statement that 'if the work used as a libretto is published as a literary work, or without reference to a particular musical setting, it may be entered under its own author'. The revision committee obviously had doubts about this ruling, as they allow the alternative of treating a libretto by rule 19B, *ie* as an independent work to be entered under its own author. There seems a parallel here with the type of material covered by rule 8A — a text and illustrations combining to make a cohesive whole. Perhaps this could also be applied to librettos. Those written specially for musical compositions could be entered under the name coming first on the title-page, while others, written as independent works, would be entered by the same criteria as for illustrated works, and illustrations with accompanying text.

Special rules
The remainder of the section on entry in AACR (1967) is devoted to special rules, covering certain specified types of publication. The types covered are legal publications, including laws; constitutions; charters; treaties; court decisions; and certain religious publications — sacred scriptures, creeds, liturgical works, etc. The existence of these special rules is disappointing as they repeat certain aspects of earlier codes, particularly ALA (1949) in providing rules for special types of publication, rather than conditions of authorship. This is what Lubetzky managed to dispense with in CCR (1960). One must suspect the influence of certain 'pressure groups' in the United States. This section also differs from the general pattern of the code by the introduction of form subdivisions, which had been eschewed by Lubetzky, but tolerated by ICCP (1961).

Rule 20 deals with laws, *ie* legislative enactments and decrees that govern political jurisdictions, and that are not covered by later, more specialised rules. This rule is interesting because it excludes all traces of an author element in the heading. Such laws or statutes are to be entered under the name of the *jurisdiction covered by the law*, followed by a form subheading *Laws, statutes, etc.* There is no author element at all in this type of heading, and the rule states quite categorically that 'if the law or decree is promulgated by a jurisdiction other than the one governed by it, make a reference from the promulgating jurisdiction followed by the subheading *Laws, statutes, etc.* and the title of the publication'. In previous codes the name of the jurisdiction was assumed to be an author element in the heading, though ALA (1949) in rule 84B (Laws of territories, dependencies, etc) inferred the same as AACR (1967). Such headings appear to the writer to be partly subject headings and partly form headings, with little or no author element in them.

Similarly, constitutions and charters of political jurisdictions are, by rule 22, to be entered under the name of the jurisdiction to which they apply, and not under the body granting them, but with a reference from that body. This has been the case in other codes from AA (1908), particularly for charters.

Form subheadings are again used for religious publications, (rules 27-29), for an officially sanctioned or traditionally accepted text of a religious observance, book of prayers, etc. Liturgies would be entered under the specific denominational church with the form subheading *Liturgy and ritual.* A note with the rule states that this form of subheading has been chosen because of its long-established usage. Sacred scriptures (rule 27) are, as formerly, to be entered under a uniform title. This section also differs from the others in that it does not completely separate rules for choice of heading from those of form of heading.

The section of AACR (1967) dealing with special types of publication represents a breach in the authorship principle. In effect, this section states that certain types of publication must be exempted from the basic principles of the code. This may be in fact so, but Lubetzky argued against such exceptions. Even if we accept the AACR (1967) position that such publications should be excepted, complete agreement on what all the exceptions should be is more difficult. The use of form headings or form subheadings is different from the use of title-page information, and thus this section of the code introduces a third category to the sequence — Under author; if none, under title — we must now also say — if author and title are inappropriate, under some heading manufactured by the cataloguer. To sum up, however, it might be said that Cutter, AA (1908) and ALA (1949) modified the 'intellectual

137

responsibility' principle in favour of the alleged public convenience, while Lubetzky and CCR (1960) modify the same principle in favour of title-page information.

It is certainly too early yet to pass judgement with any degree of finality on AACR (1967). Catalogue codes have to be tested against actual use in a library before they can be effectively evaluated. AACR (1967) is inevitably a compromise between the ideals of its chief architect, Seymour Lubetzky, and the economics of practical librarianship as represented by the large research libraries in the United States. This code, more than any other, is designed primarily for the card catalogue, in which many large research libraries have invested large sums of money, but AACR (1967) has been completed at a time when the card catalogue is giving way to the computer-produced book catalogue. Yet these very libraries, as represented in the United States by the Library of Congress and the Association of Research Libraries, which forced the departures from the ideals of Lubetzky in the interests of economy in their card catalogues, are the very libraries which are planning to replace their card catalogues by book catalogues produced by computer.

So far as the authorship concept is concerned, AACR (1967), in its first 32 rules, does much to advance and establish a concept of authorship based on the idea of the author as being the person or corporate body primarily responsible for the intellectual or artistic content of a work being catalogued. In this respect it goes further than most of its predecessors; indeed, it could be said that, in some instances, the attempt to solve all problems in terms of principal authorship or its absence is taken too far. This concept of authorship may be insufficient or inappropriate to solve all author cataloguing problems. AACR (1967) admits this in certain rules. In shared authorship it falls back on the first- named author on the title-page, when no · principal author is indicated, and there are not more than three. This departure from the author concept in favour of the title-page information is legitimate since it achieves a practical heading. The same situation is repeated in rule 8A where a work which is the result of collaboration between author and artist is catalogued under the first name given on the title-page. Where
138

AACR (1967) may be taken to task is in its occasional insistence on the application of the authorship principle to situations which require different treatment. We have already looked at the rule for adaptations (rule 7), where an anonymous adaptation of a well-known work would be entered under title, and not the original author. A much more practical heading would have resulted from the application of the principle of 'the name most permanently associated with the work'. This principle is invoked elsewhere in certain cases of works many times revised, but where the original author's name is still prominently associated with the work by being given at the beginning of the title on the title-page.

In deriving headings for certain special types of publication, for example texts of laws in rule 20, AACR (1967) ignores considerations of authorship altogether, as we have already noticed, in favour of a heading which can only be described as a subject heading with a form subdivision.

Lubetzky's ideals were finally shattered at the Miami Conference of the American Library Association in 1962, when LC and ARL forced alterations in the rules to avoid too many changes in their catalogues. C Sumner Spalding, who succeeded Lubetzky as editor, was left to put together the pieces of the ideal as best he could.

It is ironic that the Americans whose CCR (1960) did much to ensure the success of ICCP (1961) should now find themselves having to repudiate some of its principles. In this country we are in a different situation; the national library has always used its own code of rules, and the British National Bibliography does not have its own catalogue to maintain. Consequently the BNB promptly adopted AACR (1967) as from January 1968. The editors of the British text have not had to adopt the compromises of the Americans, and in this respect the British text is a more genuine successor to Lubetzky, CCR (1960) and ICCP (1961).

12
COMPUTERS AND CATALOGUING RULES

Much current activity in cataloguing is concerned with the application of computers to the production of catalogues. At first computers have been used as printing and up-dating devices. The ability of the computer to handle and collate large masses of data accurately and speedily makes it eminently suitable for this purpose. The next stage in this development which is already upon us is the use of the data-store of the computer as the catalogue itself to be questioned by on-line access. The computer offers the opportunity to list bibliographical items under numerous bibliographical tags, which would be quite .impossibly uneconomic using manual records. In the computer store a bibliographic item can be recorded under as many identification tags as may be thought necessary — author, title, date, publisher, printer, etc, etc, and any or all of these tags can be used to recall the bibliographic descriptions of the items concerned. This is only possible if the various fields of information on a full catalogue entry are fully tagged and identified at the input stage. One can isolate two distinct types of fields of data on a catalogue record:

1 Those parts of a catalogue entry which remain constant, *eg* title, imprint, collation, etc.

2 Those parts of the entry which may vary, *eg* author heading, added entry headings for subsidiary authors, class numbers for different classification schemes, or even for the same scheme, subject headings, etc.

The division of the information found on a catalogue entry into these two types of field gives added importance to the title statement. It is invariable, and not open to the different interpretations that a main author heading is. From this point
140

of view the distinction between main and added entries loses its significance. Main and added entry headings become merely alternative 'tags' for the same record. The title assumes an added importance and becomes the standard and invariable unit of identification for a bibliographical item. If the title is not used for identification purposes, a substitute could be found in a standard numbering system for bibliographical items, such as the British National Bibliography number or the Standard Book Numbering System in this country, the latter being so designed to be able to incorporate numbers from other countries as well, particularly the United States of America.[1] The Marc tape record will store its information by SBN number for each discrete bibliographical unit and access to each item will be by SBN.[2]

With the development of efficient and versatile character reading devices, the title of a bibliographical item again assumes importance. In the scanning of a title-page by such devices the sequence of the items as they are scanned assumes importance, and here, again, the title almost invariably appears before the name of the author on title-pages. Moreover, as we have seen in the preceding study of the cataloguing codes, the name of the person printed on a title-page is not necessarily that chosen for entry, and the presence of more than one personal name on a title-page, in, for example, multiple authorship, adds importance to the order of the names as they appear on a title-page. Again, the order of names on a title-page may not correspond to the order of choice of name as given in existing codes of rules for author entry.

It may be objected that 'main entries' will still be needed for single-access catalogues, such as union catalogues. This is not necessarily so. It seems more than likely that such catalogues will be stored on computer tape or discs, and the individual items will be identified and arranged by a number rather than by an author or other type of identification tag. The number could be supplied by the BNB or SBN numbers already referred to. This would facilitate the arrangement of the entries, a

1   The Standard Book Numbering Agency. Standard book numbering. London, 1967.
2   British National Bibliography. Marc record service proposals. June, 1968. (BNB Marc documentation service publications, No.1).

computer being geared to the handling of numerical rather than alphabetical data, and would also aid access to bibliographic items.

Even without the advent of computers, there has been a tendency to regard the title of a bibliographical item as a more satisfactory identification tag than a main author heading, *vide* A J Wells's statement at the Brasenose Conference on Automation in 1966:

> In many ways it would be easier to plan a catalogue record which began with the title, for this would dispense with the notion of a main entry heading – a notion which has occupied more of our time to little purpose than everything else in librarianship except, perhaps classification and subject indexing. There is little doubt in my mind that we could get international agreement on a standard format for a machine-readable catalogue record if we dispensed with the necessity for a main entry heading.[1]

Also from Wells at Brasenose:

> I would like to hope that one of the outcomes of this conference will be the setting up of an international committee to establish not a new code for a heading, but an international standard for the contents of a catalogue record, and this of course would have significant space for traditional handling as well as for machine use. The problem of main entry heading is, I believe, insolvable along the lines we have been pursuing. The reason lies in the fundamental fallacy of the notion of a main entry heading. Books are sought by different people using different factors. Behind our union catalogues we have to have our multi-access catalogues.
>
> The function which we are at present trying to make the main entry perform would be done by some such device as a book number.[2]

1 The Brasenose Conference on the Automation of Libraries. Proceedings . . .; edited by John Harrison and Peter Laslett, London, 1966, pp 24-25.
2 Ibid, p 30.

142

The same movement away from the concept of a main entry for each bibliographical item in a catalogue was evident in the deliberations of the Descriptive Cataloguing rules Sub-Committee of the Library Association. This concept probably lies at the root of the major differences in rules for description between the two texts of AACR (1967). If the basic catalogue record for an item were to be regarded as title, imprint and collation, with the appropriate headings added at the top of each entry in the catalogue — author, subject, series, etc, the problem of main entries would disappear and much more flexibility could thus be introduced into the catalogue. By our present method of unit entry, the main entry heading, once having been chosen, will always appear as the second element on all added entries for the same book. For added author entries, at least, this can lead to considerable difficulties in filing. The presence of this main author heading also dictates that the sequence of added entries under a subject heading will be an alphabetical one by author. In many instances a chronological sequence may be more appropriate. This would be quite possible provided we dispense with the inevitability of the main entry heading appearing immediately after the added entry heading.[1]

It is of some interest that Charles Coffin Jewett, to whom we have previously alluded, designed his stereotype plates on the basis of unit entry under title, leaving individual libraries to fill in their own headings. Our previous reference to Jewett as being in advance of his age is reinforced by this observation.

In a recent article in the *Journal of documentation* F H Ayres also advocates title entry in connection with AMCOS (Aldermaston Mechanised Cataloguing and Ordering System), and the computer handling of bibliographical data.[2] He claims not only that the sorting problems with a title file are much less than with an author file, but also that a title catalogue with an author index would result in more efficient identification of bibliographic items than the more conventional author catalogue. He backs up his arguments with the results from

1   A E Jeffreys. Alternative headings. *Catalogue & index* (8) October 1966, 4-5.
2   F H Ayres. Author versus title: a comparative study of the accuracy of the information which the user brings to the library catalogue. *Journal of documentation.* 24 (4) December 1968, 266-272.

a small survey of 450 requests in a special library. The sample is rather small for making generalisations, as Ayres himself admits, but it reinforces the impression that current cataloguing thought is moving away from the author/title approach in the direction of the title catalogue.

13
SUMMARY AND CONCLUSIONS

What conclusions can be drawn from this historical analysis of the concept of authorship in the major cataloguing codes in the English language over the last century and a quarter? Is there any thread of development towards a better understanding and solution of the problems involved? It is difficult to see any such progress. In many respects, the earliest code, the British Museum code, is as modern as any of its successors. It is a pragmatic, practical code designed for a specific purpose, to aid cataloguers contributing entries for thegreat *General catalogue of printed books.* It was formulated by one of the greatest cataloguers of all time, Sir Anthony Panizzi. The rules themselves were firmly based on the information to be found on the title-page of the book being catalogued. In this it is modern. The subsequent evolution of codes of cataloguing rules was generally away from the title-page information towards a more theoretical heading. It is unfortunate that after Cutter the making of codes for author cataloguing came into the hands of the legalists rather than the pragmatists like Panizzi and Cutter. This state of affairs held good from the first decade of the present century until the publication of Andrew Osborn's 'The crisis in cataloging' in 1941. Even then this was too late for the subsequent ALA (1949). It took a combination of circumstances to alter the situation:

    1 The backlogs of cataloguing existing in many of the larger libraries, particularly on the American continent.

    2 The costs of cataloguing, particularly by AA (1949) were finally appreciated by library administrators.

    3 The unsatisfactory nature of some of the cataloguing

145

produced by the application of AA (1908) and ALA (1949).

4 On the American continent, the influence of the Library of Congress's printed card scheme, and the economies effected therein.

5 The logic and single-mindedness of Seymour Lubetzky in pursuing his ideal of a code of cataloguing rules based on logical principles of entry as required by certain bibliographical conditions.

That we are not entirely free from tradition even with AACR (1967) can be seen in the concessions which the American text has had to make to the inertia of the larger research libraries in the United States.

One might be excused for forming the opinion that time was on the side of the cataloguers, with the apparently leisurely way in which revision of the codes has taken place. But time is now against the cataloguers. Unless we can put our house in order and produce a practical and logically defensible code of rules, we may find that we have been overtaken by the systems analyst and the computer programmer. It is they who are the contemporary image of twentieth-century society, and not the cataloguer sitting in a back-room of a library. Unless cataloguers and computer experts can achieve some sort of 'modus vivendi' of mutual benefit, we may find ourselves forced to accept standards and practices which we find repugnant. Our best insurance against this happening is to demonstrate that our catalogues are based on practical sense and sound logic.

SELECT BIBLIOGRAPHY

ALLEN, Thelma E and DICKMAN, Daryl Ann. New rules for an old game. London, 1968.

ANGELL, Richard S. The need for a new United States code. *Library quarterly* 26 (4) October 1956, 318-330.

AYRES, F H. Author versus title: a comparative survey or the accuracy of the information which the user brings to the library catalogue, by F.H.Ayres [and others].
Journal of documentation 24 (4) December 1968, 266-272.

BRANDHORST, W T. Corporate author cataloging and the technical report literature. *American documentation* 15 (1) January 1964, 35-47.

BUCKLAND, Laurence F. The recording of Library of Congress bibliographical data in machine form: a report prepared for the Council on Library Resources Inc, Washington, 1965.

CATALOGUING RULES: progress in code revision. *Library Association record* 62 (8) August 1960, 248-253.

CHAPLIN, A Hugh. Tradition and principle in library cataloguing. Toronto, 1966 (The Bertha Bassam lecture in librarianship no.1).

DEWTON, Johannes L. The grand illusion: some observations on the present state of cataloging and the American Library Association's Draft code. *Library journal* May 1 1961, 1719-1729.

DRAPER, Hal. How to roll back the corporate empire. *Library resources* 5 (1) Winter 1961, 73-81.

DUNKIN, Paul S. Criticisms of current cataloging practice. *Library quarterly* 26 (4) October 1956, 286-302.

FIELD, F Bernice. The new catalog code: the general principles and the major changes. *Library resources* 10 (4) Fall 1966, 421-436.

FRANCIS DOLORES, *Sister.* Canadian Committee on cataloguing principles. Cataloguing workshop, June 17 1961. Working paper no 2, choice of main entry 1961. 15p (typescript).

HOARE, P A. Cataloguing code revision: a participant's report on the Conference on cataloguing rules held at Chaucer House in May 1964. *Library association record* 67 (1) January 1965, 10-12.

INTERNATIONAL FEDERATION OF LIBRARY ASSOCIA-
TIONS. Statement of principles adopted at the ICCP,
October, 1961: annotated ed, with commentary and
examples by A H Chaplin, assisted by Dorothy Anderson;
provisional ed. Sevenoaks (Kent), 1966.
JOLLEY, Leonard. International conference on cataloguing
principles. II.Thoughts after Paris. *Journal of documentation*
19 (2) June 1963, 47-63.
The principles of cataloguing. London, 1961.
KEBABIAN, Paul B. The Chaplin report: a symposium.
Library resources 8 (3) Summer 1964, 213-228.
LIBRARY ASSOCIATION. *Library Research Committee.*
Cataloguing Rules Sub-Committee. Report on the
Conference on cataloguing rules, May 1964. 1964. 13p
(typescript).
LUBETZKY, Seymour. Catalog code revision. *Library journal.*
December 15 1964, 4863-4865, 4870.
Development of cataloging rules. *Library Trends.* 2 (2)
October 1953, 179-186.
MILLER, John F. Sic transit Lubetzky: an intemperate look at
the Anglo-American cataloguing rules: *APLA Bulletin* 31 (2)
May 1967, 55-56.
OSBORN, Andrew D.Cataloging and cataloging codes in other
countries today. *Library quarterly* 26 (4) October 1956,
276-285.
The crisis in cataloging. *Library quarterly* 9 (4) October 1941,
393-411.
PETTEE, Julia. The development of authorship entry and the
formulation of authorship rules as found in the Anglo-
American code. *Library quarterly* 6 (3) July 1936, 270-290.
PIGGOTT, Mary, *ed.* Cataloguing principles and practice: an
inquiry. London, 1954.
ROSENTHAL, Joseph A. The administrative implications of the
new rules. *Library resources* 10 (4) Fall 1966, 437-444.
RUYSSEN, Yvonne *and* HONORE, Suzanne. Corporate authors
and the cataloguing of official publications; translated by
Elizabeth Fudakowska. *Journal of documentation* 13 (3)
September 1957, 132-146.
TAIT, James A. The Anglo-American cataloging rules, 1967.
Library review 21 (2) Summer 1967, 69-74.

TAUBE, Mortimer. The cataloging of publications of corporate authors. *Library quarterly* 20 (1) January 1950, 1-20.

TAUBER, Maurice F. ALA rules for entry: the proposed revolution! *Journal of cataloguing and classification* 9 (3) September 1953, 123-142.

WATKINS, David R. A reference librarian's view of the Draft cataloging code. *Library journal* May 1 1961, 1730-1733.

WRIGHT, Wyllis E. A report of progress on catalog code revision in the United States. *Library quarterly* 26 (4) October 1956, 331-336.

INDEX

Note: The explanation for the abbreviations of the names of codes will be found on p6.

151

152

Literary unit 14-15.

Marc tapes 141.
Maunsell, Andrew 17.
Medieval catalogues 16.
Mediumistic writings. *ALA (1949)* 82.
Monastic libraries 16.
Multiple authorship 11-12; *AA (1908)* 52-63; *AACR (1967)* 127-135;
 ALA (1949) 79-83; *BM* 23; *CCR (1960)* 96-101; *Cutter* 41-43;
 ICCP (1961) 116-117.
Music. *AA (1908)* 60-61.

National institutions. *AA (1908)* 71.
'No conflict' principle 20.

Panizzi, *Sir* Anthony 21.
Paris principles (ICCP 1961) 108-120.
Periodicals. *Smithsonian* 33.
Personal *vs.* corporate authorship. *AA (1908)* 65-66; *ALA (1949)* 66-67;
 AACR (1967) 132-134; *CCR (1960)* 102.
Primary responsibility, as basis for authorship. *AACR (1967)* 124; 132.
Principal author. *AACR (1967)* 124.
'Prussian instructions' 14.
Pseudonymous works. *AA (1908)* 74; *ALA (1949)* 83-85; *BM* 22; 25;
 Smithsonian 35.

References. *ICCP (1961)* 111.
Related works. *AACR (1967)* 135-136; *CCR (1960)* 98; 100.
Revisions. *AA (1908)* 59-60; *ALA (1949)* 83; *CCR (1960)* 99-100.
Royal commissions. *AA (1908)* 72.

Serials. *AACR (1967)* 130-131.
Shared authorship. *AACR (1967)* 127-128.
Smithsonian code 31-36.
Spurious works. *ALA (1949)* 86.
Standard Book Number 141.
Subordinate corporate bodies. *AA (1908)* 68-69; *AACR (1967)* 134;
 CCR (1960) 103.
Supplements. *CCR (1960)* 98; 100.

Thematic catalogues. *AA (1908)* 59; *ALA (1949)* 59.
Title, as identifying characteristic for bibliographical item 8; 141-144.
Translations. *AA (1908)* 49; *AACR (1967)* 135; *ALA (1949)* 83;
 BM 22; *CCR (1960)* 99; *Smithsonian* 35.

153

Trefler, Florian 17.

Uniform headings. *ICCP (1961)* 110-111.
Uniform titles *CCR (1960)* 99.

Variant titles. *CCR (1960)* 99.
Vocal music. *Cutter* 43.

Wheatley, H B *How to catalogue a library* 21.
Work *vs* book 13-14; 93.